DON'T JUMP TO CONCLUSIONS

Mandar Chitre

VISHWAKARMA
PUBLICATIONS VP ™

Don't Jump To Conclusions

First Edition - September 2016

© Author

ISBN - 978-93-85665-40-0

Published by:
Vishwakarma Publications
283, Budhawar Peth, Near City Post,
Pune- 411 002.
Phone No: (020) 20261157
Email: info@vpindia.co.in
Website: www.vpindia.co.in

Cover Design
Meghnad Deodhar

Typeset and Layout
Gold Fish Graphics, Pune.

Printed at
Repro Knowledgecast Limited
Thane

Dear Reader,

The Book

'Don't Jump To Conclusions' is a book for everybody. We all face difficult situations. Things don't happen the way we want them to. Life takes a turn and our plans get disturbed. At such times, we react. The reactions are strong. Then we pass judgements and reach a conclusion. All further actions now are dictated by our conclusions. We forget our main path and get diverted on to another road that should not have been taken or will never lead to the desired destination.

When we don't want to carry an umbrella, we look at the sky and conclude that it won't rain. In most such cases, we end up getting wet. The mood is spoilt. We curse ourselves. Anger leads to negative thoughts. They change our motivation levels. We then ensure that our work gets affected. Not just work, but relationships too get affected.

Such examples are very common. Most of us are aware that such conclusions end up in problems. But as human beings we keep on making mistakes. Though we may not become perfect but we can at least ensure that the major decisions of our life are not based on mistakes leading to wrong conclusions.

Even when good things happen, we pass judgements, leading to conclusions and start taking others for granted. This can sometimes lead to sorrow due to high expectations.

Therefore in both good and bad situations jumping to conclusions may not be always the best thing to do.

Leadership Stories

I appreciate your interest in reading books about leadership. As the author of this book, I want to contribute in shaping your life towards improving your thought process. With two decades of corporate experience, I want to ensure that you do not make mistakes commonly made. If you read this book and follow a particular process, I am confident it will lead to a positive change in your life.

I will also advise you to help others. This will certainly increase your learning, and that can be extremely helpful for self-improvement. It will give you a strong feeling of satisfaction as well as polish your skills and transform you into an inspirational leader. Good leaders do not create followers; they only build more leaders. I have learnt this from my ex-boss and can never forget that after all we are remembered only for our good deeds. Designations, positions, power and authority - all these are temporary. It is the relationship that remains for a longer period and helps during despondency and failures.

The "Learning Through Stories" Concept:

I thank you for choosing this book containing fictional stories on leadership. It is about people who faced challenges. They suffered a bit, but had the desire and capability to come up with solutions and finally win the race.

As children, all of us have learnt so much through stories. 'Slow and steady wins the race' is what you learnt from the story of the hare and the tortoise. 'The Thirsty Crow' taught you to add pebbles to the pot containing water at an unreachable level. We are sure that all those who are paying EMIs can relate to this story. Even a small mouse could help the lion go free from the hunter's net. Each story had a moral for imparting to us a fundamental lesson that experience in life teaches us.

My idea is to continue this effective childhood learning style. The concept is the same for my book. I suggest that you read each story and think about it. Try to relate it to your life. Check if you currently face a similar problem or have been in a similar situation in the past. The problems are not difficult, but people are unable to see light at the other end of the tunnel. If you just sit back, relax and let your thoughts follow, solutions are bound to emerge.

The trick is to ask the right questions after reading each story and be a good reader. It will open your mind with solutions automatically evolving. Solutions offered in my stories may not be the best and I am sure that you will come up with far better ones. But it is important to generate a thought process in the right direction.

The Game of Life

Sometimes I feel that life is a game - Snakes and Ladders. Nobody can ever remove the snakes. They will always be there. Try to stay away as much as possible, but a few of them will still do their job by pulling you down. The solution is very simple. You have to keep a close watch on them. My book does not provide solutions against the existence of snakes but it will certainly help you convert ladders into springs. The springs will help accelerate your growth and repair harm done by the snakes. A few right springs can lead to a jumpstart. Once you get used to the springs, those snakes will no longer matter.

I always wanted to write a book but couldn't think of a good subject. While counselling others I realised that so many people in the corporate world are unable to see a danger approaching and eventually end up wiping out their own existence from an organisation. In the current business scenario, all jobs are somewhat unsecured. If you say "no" to your boss, s/he will soon find somebody who will do it better than you and that too, on a lower pay-packet.

Flow of information due to improved technology is faster. Businesses need continuous improvements. This generates the need to make changes. Changes bring ups and downs that can lead to addition or deletion of job profiles. A sudden shifting of gears within an organisation leads to instability that employees find difficult to handle.

This book is about those leaders who faced difficulties, managed to conquer them and then worked hard to succeed. The book has nine short stories. Each story contains a unique challenge and has a Lesson that can be carried forward.

My Suggestions

For the reader of this book, it is important to read only one story at a time. Then it is important to ponder over and assess if the solution implied and suggested by the story's Lesson can be utilized and applied. Make some notes at the end of each story. it is finally your decision to choose the best solution.

All stories are fictional and resemblance of any kind to any person, living or dead, would be sheer coincidence.

I dedicate this book to my bosses, friends, competitors and colleagues who taught me the good, the bad, the ugly and even some evil things. Their contribution to my life has been extremely important.

Also special thanks to my wife, son, parents, sister, nephew and niece, to whom I could not give sufficient time.

As part of the CKP Chamber of Commerce and Industry, I sincerely recommend this book to all budding businessmen and professionals.

I thank the entire Walplast family for their significant contribution and for teaching me many important lessons.

Foreword

I have read many books on leadership & management. It is certainly a vast subject which is continuously evolving for development of the human capital. Across the globe, authors are working on adding innovative ways of developing talent.

'Don't Jump To Conclusions', is certainly a good read. I like the idea of learning through reflections, with the base of storytelling.

The stories of this book are thought provoking. The idea of reading only one story at a time & getting into a thinking mode is certainly going to help the readers.

It is difficult but not impossible to think positive during failures. It is a critical phase where you will need to take tough decisions. Life will always have challenges & you need to be strong enough to handle failures positively. The stories in this book have demonstrated some of these fundamentals very nicely.

Mandar Chitre has been an old friend. I appreciate his noble attitude & innovative way of helping others. He is confident that the readers will be able to take benefit from this book in the business world. Not just business, but even in the personal life, Mandar's book will help to develop, grow & spread happiness.

I wish for success to all the readers of this book & to Mandar for achieving his mission.

Manish Chopra
Senior Vice President
Global Risk Leader

TABLE OF CONTENT

The Car

It was a happy Friday afternoon and everybody in the office was focused on making weekend plans. This usually happens in a well-established, technically advanced multinational, where people sometimes work if they get time from gossiping and browsing the net. Highly overstaffed and well defined processes with customers coming back for superior technology makes life at the workplace easy and comfortable. Five-star stays, frequent flier miles, couple of training programs every year, luxury cars etc., are features common to top employees. Cost-cutting or cost-reduction is not in the picture at all. Life is a piece of cake for these employees. Most of them aren't ambitious enough and happily participate in low stress work activities followed by mouth-watering company lunches, desserts, tea breaks and a peaceful life. These people are known as "soft-toys of the corporate world."

Ravi was not a soft toy. He was extremely ambitious and gunning to move up towards the top-most chair. He took extra efforts to increase business. His energy and efforts were recognised by his bosses who had just promoted him from Assistant Sales Manager to Head, Logistics Department. Ravi was part of the ambitious cross functional job rotation project designed for specially chosen talented employees. He usually spent Friday afternoons in planning the next week. The trip to Delhi needed a lot of pre-work. The case was complicated and it would need lots of negotiations to convert the problem into an amicable solution. Dedication was his middle name and he always thought that nothing could change his attitude and ambition to reach the top. Sometimes the biggest boss of the world, the Almighty, plays a game with us just to check if we are strong or weak. This is exactly what happened to our story's hero.

"Ping" was the sound followed by an email from the HR department. It came with a special tag, indicating changes in policy decisions and has reference to the HR manual. Friday afternoon was the best time to send critical emails on policies that may generate reactions from employees. They always believe that most of the employees do not check emails on Friday afternoons and even if they did, the effect could cool down a little over the weekend. For active employees, such emails are a "first to see" types.

Ravi quickly went carefully through it, word by word and got a 440 volt shock that made him almost fall from his chair. 'How can they do it?, are they idiots?', he thought. As he read it once again, the picture became crystal clear. His mind turned blank. The whole world came to a stand-still. Sometimes it happens that tears roll, but only inside; the heart bleeds within, but blood doesn't ooze outside. This email brought extreme pain to Ravi for whom life was over and he started to hate the company. It was a disaster and a decision taken by the HR and policy committee without taking repercussions into account..

His next big worry was how he would be able to inform the family and would they be able to take the shock. "Will the son still respect his father? What will the mother-in-law say?" "His status in the housing society will dip very low," so many thoughts started to run through his mind.

Readers, let me make it clear that Ravi had not been sacked. It was just a minor change in the car policy of the company that did not affect more than 10% of the company's employees. ROCE was in trouble. ROCE is Return On Capital Employed by the promoters of the company based in Europe. They had great expectations from India and China. The pressure was to ensure better returns from these countries. This was a simple change which seemed to be logical and in line with industry norms. The company offered a vehicle to the top three levels of the managerial grade. Each level had been offered a car of a certain value. Once an employee got a company car, it was replaced with a new one every five years. During these five years, even if the employee was promoted to the next level, his/her car would be replaced only after five years. Then the employee could opt for the next level car as per the promotion. If not promoted and in the same grade, it would be just a replacement of the same car model.

The company's managing director had a five year term and the new Managing Director decided that the car policy was important to retain the top performing employees but it was not necessary to spend more in the non-sales category. This would help ease pressure on ROCE. The sales team travels a lot and visits customers, therefore it was logical to provide it with high-end cars, however for other managers, a car was used only for travelling to the office and they could use a lower end car as a special benefit. The policy was about employee retention and technically salesmen were critical positions. The policy appeared logical and was quickly accepted by the committee who always tried to get on to the good side of the new Managing Director. Ravi was now in a senior but non-sales position. Therefore it had hit him hard.

Each policy change transforms employees into three categories, the beneficiaries, the neutrals and the losers. Ravi in this case topped the list of losers. Five years ago, when he had got a chance to enter the sales team, he danced with joy because the company then offered him a brand new Maruti Alto (costing Rs.300,000) and he was also blessed with a child. Life had become beautiful because Ravi was now a father with a car and a nice job. Ravi decided to give his best to the company and put in his 100%. Time flew and business grew to such an extent that in five years, Ravi was promoted twice. He was now listed in the talent pool of the company and was being considered to actually head the Logistics Department with special training provided from the best institutes.

Now to explain the tragedy - we take you back by a month when the Maruti Alto had completed five years and Ravi was given permission to upgrade his car. With his new grade, he was now eligible to the next level of a car and he selected the top end model of Ford Fiesta (Rs.800,000) with leather seats and superior features. The car's quotation was sent to HR for processing. His case was clear and they said the company would process his application and release a Purchase Order to the car showroom in a few days. Ravi announced this to his family who were thrilled and they all reached the showroom to take a test drive of the Fiesta. The courteous salesman explained each feature of the car and they jointly decided to select the colour platinum with the latest 6-CD changer music system. Wishes had become horses and Ravi was riding with great ease toward success. However as per the current policy, this car could be given only to the sales team and not to the Head of the Logistics Department who would have to select a lower level car. He therefore was eligible for a car worth Rs.500,000. If this policy had come a few weeks before, the pain would definitely have been a lot less.

The phone rang. It was Ravi's best friend Chirag. This is what you call a friend in need, thought Ravi.

"Hello Ravi, I have some great news, you will dance with joy" Chirag was excited.

"Hello Chirag, how are you? Tell me what you have been doing!" Ravi was struggling with words.

"You will not believe this, I've just purchased a new Honda City with the profits I made on the last deal, isn't it awesome? We can now go to great pubs and get off in style. Let's meet, I will take you to the showroom, we will take delivery together, and have lots of fun" said Chirag.

"Wow!" said Ravi, but the "wow" was not real. Chirag however was not in a position to understand the difference between a real and fake 'Wow'.

Ravi's blood was boiling. He felt a strong wave of anger. He suddenly realised that circumstances can sometimes lead you to want you to kill your best friend. He was not too sure about God, but the Devil definitely existed in this world. "Chirag had his own trading business and could pile up so many things to reduce his declared income, curse the laws of the land," thought Ravi. "I slog like a donkey and pay more tax than all the petty businessmen in my building," Ravi continued to think in a disgruntled fashion.

"Great, Chirag, Heartiest Congratulations, we will surely celebrate, what colour did you select? I hope it matches your personality" Ravi was trying to build a conversation.

"Steel-grey, manly and solid, I'm sure you'll love it, just paid Rs.900,000 great deal I must say. I was also thinking about some more expensive cars but one should be careful not to invest too much" Chirag was in a great mood, talking non-stop.

"Ok buddy, I got to continue my meeting, let's talk later" Ravi could not bear it any longer and cut the line although he would have preferred cutting Chirag's throat.

"What a great Friday evening it was, the whole world celebrating and I am moving towards sadness, humiliation, frustration and jealousy and also planning to murder my best friend," Ravi was really down.

Starting his old car, the radio station picked up a nice song for him from the famous movie "Anand", "zindagi kaisi hai paheli haye, kabhi to hasaaye, kabhi ye rulaye." (Life is a puzzle, it sometimes makes you laugh and sometimes cry). The Alto negotiated the evening traffic and reached him home with the door opening with his wife's dialogue, "So how are the last few days in the Alto doing?".

"Stop it, I am too tired for it" he gave a low reaction.

"You are always tired when it comes to family. On Monday morning, you will be all fresh and energetic for the office. There is no family life for you" she was constantly nagging him.

Wives of performing managers always have a problem complaining that their husbands do not give enough time to the family. But they also love them for being at a respectable position in the office.

He was silent and told her that he was too tired for anything. He pushed some dinner into his mouth and crashed into his bed. Most husbands think that they can hide everything at home, but wives have superior microprocessors coupled with the most advanced sensors. The wife could see the lines on his forehead, but decided to let it cool off and not spoil a nice weekend. She was aware that he was facing tension in the office, but this look was completely different. Some nights are long, dark, cold and sleepless. On his bed, Ravi lay in silence, with his eyes shut but a mind greatly agitated and worried.

The sky was cloudy, he saw Chirag getting out of a Mercedes; they had made him the Managing Director of the company where Ravi worked. Chirag had the Devil as his assistant and he laughed at Ravi, who was tied to his chair. The HR head was ensuring that the ropes were tight. Chirag came near him and said, "I am bringing a new policy, no more cars for managers, everybody uses only bicycles," Ravi could not tolerate this and shut his eyes. "Don't just sleep," said Chirag and the HR head together, "Wake up, wake up, wake up" they were shouting. "No, no," shouted Ravi, he was in bed, his wife was seated at his bedside and asking him to wake up, "its 8.30, you will miss your morning badminton." It was just a dream, thought Ravi, rubbing his eyes.

"Oh, what a horrible dream I have had!" he murmured.

"Stop eating spicy food" said the wife and went to the kitchen to make tea for him. A dull weekend was to follow with a lot of chores to be completed. 'Poor me' thought Ravi, "now even my dreams are getting to be horrible."

His wife handed him a list of chores. From repairing shelves, getting the grocery and fixing the child's project, she had lot of work assigned to poor Ravi. He somehow struggled through the weekend, which seemed to last longer than a month.

Monday morning he took a flight to Delhi and put his mind on the northern distributor issues. The meeting did not go well and Ravi could not focus on the negotiations. It was the first time that he was not able to conclude a deal and they had to just agree on continuing with the same status. His colleagues were now seeing a completely different Ravi. A disengaged Ravi, who was just not the same as before and they all thought that "Sir must be sick."

The only thing on Ravi's mind was the car. While in the road, his eyes just kept looking at cars. Each car smiled at him and the luxury cars seemed to be mocking him. The traffic was talking to him and teasing and taunting him that he was a big loser. The taxi driver was talkative; he started explaining to Ravi about the new music system he had installed in his car with imported speakers.

"How is the effect sir?" he asked Ravi "it is the most expensive music system and I've had it installed especially for my passengers."

"Terrible!" was going to be Ravi's answer, but he decided to play along and praised the music system. They say that when you want to achieve something desperately, the entire universe tries to deliver it to you. The driver told him how he could manage the finance to buy the expensive system. He was continuously talking about his victory.

Ravi thought that the reverse of this theory was also true. When you have an issue bothering you all the time, the whole world starts teasing you, making your life more miserable.

The evening appeared to be better because he was out of the office and had a different person with no discussions on work.

That evening he was scheduled to meet his old hostel friend Manish, now a high profile executive in a very large US multinational. Manish was always a good leader and very good at resolving fights and quarrels at the hostel. He was Ravi's roommate and they both had been through a difficult first year with class assignments, drawing submissions and exam tensions. Friendship that develops during life in a hostel stays for a lifetime. Ravi and Manish met in the local bar at Gurgaon. They both spoke about the adventures of hostel life. The first part of the discussion was on the girls they had known in college. They referred to each girl, connecting her beauty with associated memories. Men do like to remember such lost opportunities. Such discussions always end with the statement, "anyway whatever happens is for the best;" "good that we got married to the right girls."

"So, it is going to be the regular vodka for you?" said Manish.

"Yes my friend, some things should never change" replied Ravi.

After four vodkas, Ravi popped up his frustrations with Manish and expressed his hatred for the company. He called the management a heartless slave driver requesting Manish to look out for a good opportunity in Delhi. He narrated the entire story to Manish, who listened patiently. Manish who was a seasoned player and emotionally stronger than Ravi was still sober after four rounds and ordered the fifth with some more chicken kebabs. He allowed Ravi to recount his ordeal so that he could think of a good solution. It was his special style -maturity as well as attitude - a superb combination that had helped him climb the ladder in his organisation. Manish understood that Ravi had been a victim of a very common disease called "expectation". This disease infects everybody and those who are unable to keep it under control, become victims. These victims then fall into a permanent illness of sorrow and suffering. But informing Ravi directly would not be an effective way. He therefore came up with an explanation.

"So Ravi, old chap, tell me, how many hours make a day?" said Manish.

"Manish you drunken fellow, stop asking such questions. I think you should also stop drinking. You are growing old now" replied Ravi.

"First give me an answer!" shouted Manish.

"Okay, okay, there are 24 hours, stop drinking now Mani boy. Shall we order the main course?" Ravi asked.

"No, not yet, I want to drink more. Ok, now tell me the effective number of hours that we have, or the usable hours of our day" continued Manish "how much time at work, at travel, at home, at sleep etc. I want you to subtract all that non-productive time"

"Okay, let me see" said Ravi "I sleep, travel to work, take a bath, office hours, so total enjoyment time is very little. Such a cruel world!" cried Ravi.

"No, no, be specific, tell me the numbers" Manish insisted.

"Well to be specific, I sleep for 7 hours, bathroom takes 1 hour, commuting to work takes 2 hours, 1 hour in meals, okay so that gives me effective 13 hours" said Ravi.

"What do you do with your effective 13 hours?" asked Manish.

"I am usually at office for 10 hours. So the remaining 3 hours are spent at home. This would be my average daily free time that I spend with the family and relax with a book or TV" replied Ravi.

Very soon, Ravi realised that he actually spent more time at work than at home. Seven hours of sleep, plus one in the bathroom, two hours of travel, ten hours in the office, only three hours of TV and reading remaining. Therefore only 12.5% of the total time was spent on self, wife and kids. Considering that he spent time on travelling sometimes on Saturday morning or Sunday evenings, he calculated that it was not more than 10% of quality time that he got to spend with his family.

"Cruel life, cruel world, cruel office, bloody cruel policies!" Ravi was getting drunk.

"How much do you love your wife?" asked Manish "no, don't give me that reaction. I want an honest answer and I am pretty serious."

"Of course, I love her more than anything in the world. Nobody can love her more than I do!" Ravi was now high because of the alcohol.

"Are you loyal to her, will you make sacrifices for her?" asked Manish.

"Don't ask stupid questions. I love her so much that I'll do anything for her" said Ravi

"Will you pardon her if she makes a mistake?" Manish was enjoying this discussion.

"Yes, I will, I will pardon her for any mistake she makes. She is so precious to me that I can sacrifice any necessity in the world to be with her always!" Ravi was finding it difficult to gather words.

The next statement that came with the bottoms-up of the fifth shot actually stung Ravi. Initially, Ravi could not connect with what Manish was saying and how the logic was true. As the blood flowed into his brain, the situation became clearer.

Manish said "10% time is to the wife and 40% time is to the company. Love and sacrifice should be logically more towards the company than to the wife, isn't it old boy?"

A tight slap on the face was the effect of this statement. It was a classic theory which says that your work is actually a larger consumer of your time than your family. It is also important to make sacrifices and accept the decisions of your second wife, which is your organisation. Just like you promptly listen to your first wife, the second wife actually takes more of your time. Therefore, logically, your devotion, faith and love to the second wife should be at least equal. The company gives you money, knowledge, experience, opportunities to socialize, helps you increase your friends' circle, gives you status, helps you connect with other companies, gives you exposure to countries and cultures beyond India, takes care of you during sickness, pays for your medical insurance, helps you save for retirement, provides a virtual guarantee while processing a home loan or personal loan, teaches you about leadership etc. It is actually the second wife who contributes more than the first. We always make so many sacrifices for our wife, then why can't we accept a policy that isn't in our favour? Ravi's mind started churning.

He gave a smile, broad enough for Manish to understand that his concept-selling skills were way above average.

Yes, the company had given him much more than expected and this policy was just a small stab of pain he could and logically should accept. He was convinced that the company policy should be accepted.

"Manish, you have opened my eyes. I feel normal now. It is like a feeling that comes after the storm is over. I am also fully convinced because of your logic" Ravi was smiling.

"No problem my friend, I will always be there for you" said Manish. The party continued late into the night. The next day, the Delhi office saw a completely different Ravi who tackled all problems in half a day before taking the flight back home.

The team saw the change. Ravi was back in action. They gossiped about his dull day and blamed the harsh weather for his low energy. But the visit was successful and the issues had been successfully resolved.

The next issue was a bigger one that included convincing the family who had taken great pleasure in the test ride of the top-end model. The sanctioned amount was just right to buy a Ford Ikon, priced Rs.500,000. Therefore Ravi would have to approach the same showroom. It was also a painful job to visit the same showroom and from the most expensive model to now book the cheapest car..

His ego was crumbling. It was going to be extremely difficult. Ravi was nervous. It was his pride that was now at stake. The family would certainly react to this shocking news.

We are most of the time living for others. We think about others more than ourselves. "What will the world think? What will others say about me? What image will I create in society?" these questions actually dictate our life and sometimes make us do what we don't want to or don't have to.

A convinced person is determined; when there is determination it generates courage and courage leads to taking the bull by its horns. Ravi, on returning to his office, called the showroom manager and informed him of his new decision to move from the top-end Fiesta to the cheapest car which was the Flair in a budget version.

"But sir, we have already placed an order for you. How can you suddenly change?" questioned the manager.

"Sir, we have not given you the Purchase Order," said Ravi, "Don't worry I am sure you will get a better customer for the car you have ordered. Keep a positive attitude, my friend."

"I agree Mr. Ravi, but you have reduced my sales target achievement by 2 lakhs, it will reduce my incentive. I had made promises to my family. Can you please change your decision and buy the same top-end car?" asked the showroom manager.

"My dear friend, life is full of challenges - you need to accept them as God's wish. Continue the hard work and I am sure you will be successful," said Ravi.

That evening he returned home with a smile and sat down on the bed with his wife. It was still an uncomfortable situation. His heart was beating very fast.

He cleared his throat and said "I have some bad news and hope that you will understand my situation."

"You have blood sugar now, when did you do the medical test? You did not even inform me!" the wife reacted, stressfully continuing, "Why do you hide your problems from me?"

"No my dear, no sugar, no blood pressure, no medical problems to me or anybody else" said Ravi.

"Thank God, then the news is not that bad" said the wife "You have got a transfer, which city are we going to?"

"No, no, not a transfer, but still, bad news" said Ravi.

"Oh dear, you've lost your job, don't worry, we have lots of savings, I will take tuitions at home. We can sell the gold. Six months will be okay. I am sure till then you will manage to find a new job. We can manage by cutting costs." She was unstoppable.

"Relax, baby!" said Ravi.

"No, you just don't worry, I will…."

"Hold it, stop please" said Ravi "Oh just listen to me, the car policy has changed and I am now eligible for a Ford Flair and not the model of which we took the test ride. So we will get a lower version car. It is a total disaster."

He explained everything to her about the new policy decision and its effect on the company's employees.

She looked confused and then started off with some intelligent questions.

"Does our new car have an air-conditioner?" she asked

"Yes" said Ravi

"Does it have good boot and storage space? Does it have a music system?"

"Well, yes" replied Ravi.

"I hope we can get an opportunity to select the colour of our choice?" she continued.

"Yes, yes. Don't ask stupid questions" Ravi was irritated.

"Then what is the problem?" she asked

"Don't you understand, the model difference explains the status in the society, we are in trouble - don't you get it my dear?" said Ravi.

It did not make any sense to her. But she did not stop at this, her attack continued.

"I don't understand" she said.

"It's okay, you don't understand automobiles" said Ravi.

"Five years ago" she said "when you got your first small car, I saw you dancing with joy. You were so happy. Today, you are getting a car - bigger than our current car. It is also more expensive than our current car. What is now wrong with you? What I have understood is that you are getting a sedan, a bigger car? so why are you unhappy?"

"But, you see…." said Ravi, before she kept her hand on his mouth.

"The problem is that your ego has been highly inflated just like the high-end car. You have now become a "boss". You have also started bossing around at home. Your capabilities are the same, but you have changed. You still deliver the same features to your company and therefore don't expect your price tag to go up so quickly. You yourself are a Ford Ikon but you think that you are Ford Fiesta!" She had hit the nail on the head.

"I accept that I don't understand automobiles, but I understand you very well" the wife was beyond reproach.

Her words had suddenly made a big load come off his chest. They say that behind every successful man stands a woman. Ravi was pleasantly surprised by the maturity his wife was displaying. She was wise, flexible and totally down to earth. She was right, it was probably his ego and extra expectations that had misled him to jump a greater distance than what he actually was capable of. Ravi not only agreed with this but felt that it was only due to the superior home management of his wife that he could focus on the job to deliver promotion yielding results. Suddenly the world had become a beautiful place. Birds started singing, the sky's blue became royal.

Ravi was now prepared to sit with the HR Manager, who was nervous. He knew Ravi's story. Traditionally the role of HR demands handling uncomfortable situations. But this time, the HR manager was pleasantly surprised.

"I have accepted the policy sir" said Ravi to the HR Manager. He was expecting Ravi to resist and throw a tantrum. So, can we place the Purchase Order for you? he asked Ravi in a low and polite tone. He was still not very sure if Ravi was normal or was just being sarcastic about the entire episode.

"Yes, sir, please proceed with whatever fits in with your policy," said Ravi with a smile on his face.

"I thought you were not going to accept the policy" said the HR manager.

"I am here to perform and not to fight against policies" said Ravi.

This story has a happy ending. The car came home and life continued with the same vigour as before. Just as the wife had said, it was not a bad car, had all the comforts required and had certainly more space than the earlier one. Ravi did enjoy the high power it had as well as the appreciation of their neighbours congratulating him on the new car.

Imagine what would have happened if Ravi had not managed to climb up and out from inside the ditch of the policy change. He would have remained rigid and had he not agreed to have accepted, he would have fought the company management. He would have been completely de-motivated, lost his touch at work, results would have been down, his boss would have become upset, and irritation would then have definitely followed at home, spoiling relationships. Had he refused the car he would have had to start desperately searching for a new job. Six months down, the boss might not have tolerated a frustrated employee leading to the decision of removing the rotten apple from the lot. Jobless Ravi, having no car, no job and almost a divorce-like situation, would have moved to a deep financially troubled situation, relatives would then have come in and would have started helping in with the rations, increasing suffering and humiliation.

Such things did not happen. He happily accepted the decision, cancelled his request and applied for the new lower-end vehicle. The HR team was happy to have the first acceptance of the policy. They made him a role model for others to follow. They informed his boss about the entire episode, appreciating Ravi's maturity as well as decision making. Therefore and thereafter the boss also was happy. He actually forwarded the same email to Ravi along with his appreciation.

Ravi had managed to win against his ego. Once you defeat the ego, it enables you to become a better person, a more lovable human being. Everybody likes a person without ego. They like to get associated with ego-free guys and gals. The entire department becomes happy when the leader is free of ego. A bunch of happy employees can create wonders at work.

Life moves fast. Ravi's talent, attitude and performances kept him on a high rating scale taking him higher on the corporate ladder. Soon he completely forgot this episode and started enjoying the car he had been offered. When the time came for appointment of the overall department head, Ravi was the obvious choice.

Time moves very slow in distress and moves very fast when you are enjoying life. That's why Sunday is the shortest day of the week. Five years later, both Ravi and his wife entered the car showroom once again. The last episode was almost forgotten.

"Your car keys sir," said the salesman in a white crisp uniform. He explained the features of the model. "There is no need to press the remote or use the keys, he explained, simply touching the door of a locked car with the key in your pocket will automatically unlock it, so much easier this time."

"Certainly much easier this time dear?" said the wife.

Ravi understood that she was referring to the last episode of the car's purchase. Ravi and his wife laughed together spontaneously.

"Anything wrong sir?" asked the car salesman.

"Everything is just right my friend" replied Ravi and the salesman continued chatting. He was explaining the features in detail.

The new Toyota Corolla Altis (worth Rs.18,00,000) had many features beyond their imagination and the ride was much smoother than expected.

"How is the car dear?" asked the wife "though I don't understand automobiles, but this certainly looks prettier"

"Not as pretty as you, sweetheart" said Ravi as they both laughed together once again and drove the car out of the showroom.

Notes

The Real Risk

"Assets disproportionate to income" has always been the biggest concern of rich criminals who are busy evading tax or enjoying ill-gotten benefits of corruption associated with their position. A great fear working class common people should have is "performance and profile disproportionate to income". Those readers who know what I am talking about, well, you will certainly enjoy this story. And to others who have heard this for the first time, you need to read this story and understand the seriousness of this classic fact – "performance disproportionate to income"

The business world is changing rapidly. What happened in the last decade may become obsolete in today's scenario. Every working employee at every level must keep asking himself/herself this simple question: "Am I delivering more than what I take home?" or to be very specific, "Can somebody else with half my salary, deliver a better performance than the one that I am currently delivering?" The answers to these questions could open up a big box of worries.

"Does not happen in our company," "I am the favourite employee," "It will not happen with me," "I was the top performer last year and therefore it is not applicable on me," are some of the thoughts coming to your mind right now. But let me assure you that every reader of this book, including the writer is in the same boat. So, "What do we do about it?" should be the next big question.

The answer is very simple: just take up more work or improve the speed of work. Then you needn't worry at all. Keep delivering more than what is expected from you and then live a life free of this tension. Let me narrate this fundamental idea through the story that follows:

The chilling winter of Delhi had not created the shivers that were already present in the minds of all employees of this big multinational. The top management had announced restructuring of the organisation. Five business divisions were supposed to merge into three. This could lead to retrenchment of a few employees. Ravi was the Logistics Manager and faced the probability of becoming one of them. He knew that the danger was hanging like the sword of Damocles over his head. He was a guy who always expected and was prepared for the worst although he constantly kept hoping for the best."

The lunch and tea breaks were extended with extra discussions on what would happen and more interestingly, they all wished that their rivals would lose their jobs. Ravi was a better leader and decided to take the uncertainty as part of the job.

The organisational change process in a multinational takes place in four to six months. Starting from the top it percolates to the bottom. Ravi called for a meeting of his department and informed them officially about the change. He requested the staff to keep business as usual till the next announcement. Everybody returned to work, with fear in their minds.

Though the staff agreed to continue business as usual, Ravi knew that they were uncomfortable. Everybody was disturbed. Every night they all took time before falling asleep and were constantly thinking of would happen the next day.

The leader plays a lead role in such scenarios. The team looks at him or her as a role model. They get motivated only to see the leader smile. If the leader is sad and tense, the entire department gets into a foul mood.

Under such circumstances, there was one person, Gangu, who was completely undisturbed by the "winds of change" typhoon. He was doing his job with the same regularity. His bosses, very happy with his work, trusted him and introduced him as a role model. Gangu was an ordinary warehouse loader. His job was to pick up boxes and load them into a truck. He was with the company for more than 15 years and was known to be softspoken, a person who always did his job on time. Gangu was never absent and could be relied upon. At work he was serious and during lunch he would entertain others by sharing jokes. He had joined the company 15 years ago through a labour contractor. He was just a young kid of 19 years then who had migrated to the city from a nearby village. Nobody knew much about his past or his exact educational status. He could barely read and was able only to write his name.

15 years ago, Gangu had started on a salary of Rs. 2500/- and today it had crossed Rs.16,000/- per month. This was generally equal to the salary of a fresh graduate who entered the organisation through campus placements. This increase of salary had taken place due to a higher-than-average increment every year.

That chilling winter, both these men had different feelings. Ravi was worried but Gangu was happy. This is the difference that education creates. It automatically updates you on dangers that come due to circumstances. As the organisation started chiselling away at the heavy fat, Ravi saw lots of big guns being asked to go home with small severance packages. It was a big lesson for him and he understood the fact that you need to deliver more than what you take home.

Life resumed quickly after the organizational changes and everybody started falling in line with business as usual. Workers were never under the scanner because blue-collared employees were considered to be in a low-salary zone and given special exemptions. Since this was not a process change or improvement exercise, the worker category was safe.

As winter faded and summer started to throw its heat around, business started returning to normal. Sales picked up and forecasting was positive. The company management decided to invest in promotional activities. An activity being planned was towards participating in a very big multi-location exhibition event. As Logistics Manager, Ravi was responsible for the event's logistics. There was a lot of movement in demo and display equipment. The Logistics Department had limited staff and this work was an extra burden. After checking the number of order lines each team member was handling, Ravi understood that it was not possible to load more work on to any of his subordinates. He therefore decided to take the burden upon himself and started working hands-on. This action would also help him improve the overall efficiency of the department.

Gangu was in his own world. He was mentally secure, planning to buy a small room in the local slum. This would require financial investment beyond his current capacity and therefore would need some additional funding through a loan. Getting a loan through local pawnbrokers was an expensive option. He discussed this with his wife who like him, was uneducated but extremely smart. She was a housewife and hailed from his own village. Her gossip circle was large and she kept herself abreast with the latest affairs.

"Will the company extend you a loan?" was her simple but smart question.

"I wish they would, but it doesn't look likely because I have not heard of any such policy that would meet my requirement."

Women are sharper and smarter at such times at all economic levels. She pushed the ego button and reminded him that he was the best employee, most appreciated and perfect in his work. Yes, thought Gangu and set out on a mission to convince the union leader to introduce such a scheme for the employees.

Gangu was charged up by his wife. She pushed the ego button and could generate the required courage in her husband.

"Good morning sir, I am here to make a suggestion and a request" said Gangu as he entered the union leader's office.

"Yes Ganguji, tell me" the union leader was surprised to see Gangu in such a mood for the first time.

"Sir, most of the workers and lower-salaried employees need loans. But they cannot afford these loans because of the high rate of interest. The documentation is also very difficult. I would like to suggest that you should have a system where workers can take soft loans from the company. This money can be used for their important personal needs," Gangu spoke at length with the preparation that he had done at home.

"It is a good idea, but will have to wait for the next agreement settlement" said the union leader "we have some plans but they will not be an immediate priority."

Gangu was upset because the union leader had ruled out the possibility of any such loan to him. He also did not show any interest in entertaining Gangu's requirement. "So much work, honesty and 15 years of my life, my sweat, my blood given to the company and I can't even get a soft loan, how unjust!" thought Gangu. He walked away in frustration. He started loading the boxes into the truck with a long face. The supervisor was surprised to see Gangu's new angry mood.

"What is the problem Gangu?" he asked, but Gangu did not respond. The supervisor had to probe for some time for Gangu to open up.

On understanding his sorrow, he said, "don't worry my friend, you will surely get it, after all you are the best". The supervisor did not want to break his dream. He also had work to be finished. Gangu decided to compromise and with a large heart, continued his work.

The supervisor knew that it was not possible for Gangu's dream to come true. However he did not want to make him upset. He was sure that Gangu would soon forget about this desire and return to normalcy.

As the sun set over the capital, the extra work of the big event began. Hungry as a horse at 20.30 hrs, Ravi ran to the scanner to scan some dispatch documents. The office was as empty as his stomach. Then he had to make some more photocopies before returning to the confirmation emails to the exhibition organizers. He also had to call up the customs agent and remind him of the urgent clearance from the airport required the next day. His work- list was really long. Just then the paper got jammed in the copier; he struggled to get it out but ended up hurting his hand. Blood trickled down and fell on to the floor. The First Aid kit had been locked away by Mrs. Subramanium and there was no option but to head home with a finger bleeding.

The door was opened by his wife, who looked quite upset. Ravi wondered and made a mental check whether he had forgotten anything particular that she was expecting.

"Every day you come home late, you are neglecting me, what is happening at your office?" grumbled Ravi's wife. She then saw the blood on his finger. Her grumbling increased and she made no attempt to attend to his wound.

As he started pushing the rice into his mouth over the dinner table, he explained to her the great multi-location exhibition that would be held for the next three months.

"So hire more resources. You don't have to work for the entire company" she said.

But Ravi explained to her that it was too risky and the top bosses may think that he wasn't efficient. He was determined to prove himself as a "low–cost-high-efficiency manager". If I work more than one person, they will find it difficult to lay me off. He had observed the bloodbath that had taken place during organizational changes, when high-salaried bosses with smaller profiles had got fired and they had to quit, leaving behind the keys of their big cars, taking an auto rickshaw home.

"No my dear, I just cannot afford it, we have a home-loan and need investment to support our child's education. Now pass me some more rice" said Ravi. He then crashed into bed after washing his hands. He was snoring away even before she could enter the room.

The next morning, Ravi was up early to rush towards the office with full energy. The day was full of work and a small surprise waited for him.

Gangu had understood that his voice needed to be heard by the ears of more important people. He walked into Ravi's cabin and saluted him.

"Hello Gangu," greeted Ravi "how are you? Have a seat and tell me about your work".

Ravi being naturally energetic, gave a warm welcome to any person who entered his office. He believed that a leader should be approachable by all employees no matter what their levels. This ensures high engagement levels and each problem or discomfort is brought to the surface, and can be handled and overcome before it escalates into a major hurdle. With a sudden warm welcome and burst of positive energy, Gangu could not attack Ravi. He sat down and talked about the highest dispatches of March that had all been well-managed without a single complaint, well in time before six pm. Ravi quickly understood that a good worker like Gangu was free at six and could help in scanning, photocopy work or just giving him a cup of tea. He requested Gangu to work up to a little later due to the exhibition work and personally assist him. Gangu agreed and thought that it would give him an opportunity to work closely with the Head of the Department, thereby increasing his chances of getting a soft loan.

It was a classic situation where both employees had exactly different expectations from each other. Ravi was expecting loyalty and extra dedication from his best loader. Gangu was expecting money for the extra services he was offering.

The next day, Ravi plunged himself into the documentation, phone meetings, organizing other matters, etc. After 6 pm, Gangu entered Ravi's office. He was surprised to receive work above the menial tasks he was used to performing. He had never seen a scanner or copier in all his life. Ravi gave him a quick demo on the first day so that he could pick up the basic work. Unfortunately for Gangu, after having loaded trucks for 15 years, it was a formidable task to get into a completely new activity. He would miss a page, interchange documents and scan the blank side of the page, making Ravi do it all over again. Even the tea that he prepared was the worst tea both of them had ever had. Patience and persuasion are core skills of people managers in which Ravi had an above-average score. Ravi pointed out to Gangu his mistakes and asked him to be more focused.

Days turned into weeks, but there was absolutely no improvement in Gangu's first time in-office performance. He also used to be physically tired after loading trucks for seven hours. Going home late and not having dinner with the family created discomfort for Gangu as well as his wife. She was not going to accept any extra work for Gangu without extra pay.

"So, what will you get for this work that you are doing?" she tabled her demand with the first morsel entering Gangu's mouth.

"Definitely the boss will have a plan and he will reward me suitably once the work gets over. He will also be kind enough to accede to my desire to get a soft loan. I'm sure my hard work will pay off" said Gangu.

For Ravi, his problems had skyrocketed. He was now working super-extra. He had to first complete his own work and then spend time correcting mistakes made by Gangu. In addition, he also had to ruin his tastebuds by sipping the miserable tea prepared by Gangu. "What a good–for-nothing employee is Gangu," thought Ravi. He could not understand why the company employed such incompetent workers who couldn't do anything extra. Strange is the human mind that forgets the past to quickly to jump into the present and dream about the future. The good employee Gangu had just been demoted to becoming the worst office-boy and good-for-nothing fellow. Expectations do not change even if a job-profile changes or additional responsibility is added. This point needs to be remembered by all those who plan to change departments or add more feathers to their cap.

When an employee changes his role in the organisation, or gets a promotion or a transfer, it is very important to note that the employee is expected to deliver the same results and learn new tricks faster than a machine. The excuse of being new does not last more than a few days - a period known as 'the honeymoon phase'.

Friday the 13th was the day when everything went wrong. It all began with a shipment getting misplaced, followed by the exhibition demo equipment not reaching its destination due to documentation errors. It was raining complaints from all directions. Ravi tried his best to keep cool but after he saw one of the complaint messages marked to the global Head of Logistics, the emotional balance got disturbed. Sometimes people take pleasure in humiliating others by directly elevating complaints to higher levels. Marking copies of emails should be done only if required. Service organisation leaders are trained to take complaints and resolve them with a cool head. They should not react and should stand as a buffer between the complainant and the employees. But leaders are just human beings who are prone to make mistakes even after training plus getting experience.

The same morning at Gangu's house, the wife provoked him using the subject of extra pay. Her brother's wedding was on the way and she was determined to spend to show off her little wealth. She also needed a new sari, bangles and a new watch.

"You haven't spoken to sahib yet? Why are you so scared? Are you not man enough to do it?" she yelled.

"This was it," thought Gangu. "It will be done today." He finished his morning tea with bread and left a little early to work.

Gangu was now bold and full of power. Today he was going to pop the question. He was fully confident that he was delivering a good deal better than expected. The wedding was the right time to show off wealth. It was going to increase his social status especially in his wife's family who did not like him.

By sunset, Ravi was in a mess. He wanted some old files for reference and called out to Gangu but Gangu did not respond. . Ravi called him on the intercom again and ordered him to come at once. Gangu entered his cabin and Ravi asked him to get those files.

"I need overtime for this work," Gangu said in a firm voice.

Ravi did not pay attention. He was too busy to hear anything beyond his work. There was no reaction from Ravi. He once again referred to the files that were urgently required. But Gangu did not move and stood still without any reaction.

"What happened?" Ravi was rattled to see that his inefficient worker was acting so dumb.

"Overtime sir" said Gangu "I am working extra and must be paid for this service."

"What nonsense!" yelled Ravi "Just get the goddamn files".

But Gangu did not move at all. He was firm. The decision had to be taken today. The wedding was the trigger.

"What, overtime? Ravi got furious "Overtime for making lousy tea, messing up my work, mistakes in document dispatch, you must be joking," Ravi yelled.

"You are saying that I am not working well?" asked Gangu.

"Working well, you are messing up my work you idiot. Just stop this nonsense and get me the files" Ravi's voice was now at an all time high.

"Sir, you are insulting me," said Gangu, "I am the best performer, favourite of my supervisor, and how can you make such remarks?"

"Yes, it was actually my mistake" said Ravi, "I should have never hired you for this job; you're just a good–for–nothing office boy."

"Enough!" shouted Gangu.

"How dare you shout at me?" said Ravi, "Get out!"

"This is an insult" yelled Gangu, "I will not tolerate such injustice, I will approach the union and ensure that you are thrown out of this company. 15 years of service, I know all the right people, everybody likes me, Mr. Ravi, this action of yours will be your last!"

"Just get out" yelled Ravi "Get out, get out, get out!"

Some of the late sitters came close after hearing the commotion. Gangu walked out, murmuring in his mother tongue. He was abusing Ravi on his way out.

It took only a minute for Ravi to realise that he was in deep trouble.

"Oh god, what have I done!" said Ravi.

If the union acts on Gangu's complaint, there would be serious action, a strike, lockout, disturbance etc. What would the managing director say? how would his boss react, will they all challenge his leadership, will he be asked to leave?, how will he pay his home loan, how will he get a job if the industry knows that he was fired because of his war with a worker, nobody will hire him. So many thoughts entered his mind, each like an arrow piercing him deep in the heart. He sank back in his chair, going blank. After about ten minutes, he picked up his laptop and walked out of the office without bothering about the unfinished work.

He was driving his car his mind blank. The drive had a few near miss incidents because Ravi wasn't focused on the road. The car scratched a pillar while parking. The paint got ripped. It also created a minor dent in the hood. Ravi was not at all bothered about the car and its dent. His mind was frozen over the blunder he had committed with Gangu. It was not his natural temperament. He was feeling very low.

After having his dinner, Ravi quickly got to work. He was really worried as to what would happen the next day. He had seen many managers getting fired in front of his eyes. Ravi thought that he himself would probably be the next on the list.

He first checked his bank balance through internet banking, including his fixed deposits and shares. He calculated his monthly expenditure and worked out his account and saw "cash in hand" was good enough to maintain the same lifestyle for 8 months. He then prepared a list of top contacts, people who knew him well and were at senior positions like vice presidents or directors. This list was of all influential top guns who could help him with a job or recommend him to somebody important. He also started wondering what he would do in the phase where he would stop going to the office and getting a new job. Learning German had always been on his mind. He used Google to find information on classes teaching German and their fee structures. He also thought about meeting his college professor to enquire if there were any teaching assignments. He was preparing himself toward the worst scenario. That night he underwent a unique state - a tired body but a mind that was agility and agitation personified.

Gangu returned home with pride, and was in a great mood. He had given a piece of his mind to the Department Head, had had a quick chat with the union member, informed his supervisor that he wouldn't be working the next day and had plans to approach the Managing Director with his complaint. "Ravi sir will be taught a lesson!" He asked his wife to make some sweets because it was the first day of a big victory that was assured. In most of the stories he had heard, the workers always won against the management and walked away with good compensation. His wife was proud of her husband and her dreams were close to reality.

As Ravi entered his office the next day, the supervisor and a team of other officers were already present. Ravi was nervous, but got pleasantly surprised to hear from them that they actually understood the pressure he was under and expected such a blast. Ravi was not infamous for such acts, therefore he had not been perceived guilty. But they also had sympathy for Gangu who was the local favourite. It was a tough decision and they all concluded that Ravi could just finish this matter by apologizing to Gangu, so that it would all remain within the closed walls of the Department. Ravi was also convinced that he should take it easy and accept defeat before war actually commenced.

"It happens, sir" said the supervisor "don't take it to heart. Just forgive and forget."

"You are right, I need to correct my mistake on an urgent basis" said Ravi.

He immediately made an appointment with the HR head and asked the supervisor to convince Gangu to come back to work, assuring him that Ravi would display regret for what had been done by him.

Ravi entered the HR office after a long time. A few young freshers were sitting outside with nervous faces, waiting for the interview call. He realised that only the nervous probably entered this office. He sat in front of the HR head. As the discussion began, Ravi narrated every single point honestly with details. Shree was a seasoned HR head. He immediately checked on his computer about Ravi's personal file and asked the assistant to get Gangu's records. Ravi had a blemish-free record and was considered a talent by his manager. As Ravi nervously sipped his coffee in the HR office, after fifteen minutes Shree walked in and gave him a pleasant smile.

"Mr. Ravi, you surely are in trouble" he said.

"Yes, I am aware and do not want to start a war in the Union, please let me know if I can clear this with a written apology or any other action" replied Ravi.

Then it was Shree's turn to respond. He was blunt and began to give Ravi a long lecture. "All you young managers really should make yourselves familiar with the HR systems and rules. This is a serious requirement and I will immediately fix up a training program for the same. I also wish to inform you that unskilled workers are on contractual employment and not officially part of the union. Gangu cannot take his case through the union and his contract ends after three months. Therefore you could just bring him in line by informing him to behave or quit after three months" said Shree.

Ravi had a big smile on his face, "Good Lord, what a relief!" thought Ravi.

"Thank you Mr. Shree, I am going back to my office" Ravi got up to leave.

"Hang on" said Shree, "I said you are in trouble, you haven't heard me out yet."

"I didn't get you sir, I thought you said ..... " Ravi was about to continue when Shree stopped him.

"As per company policy, the rule is to keep changing unskilled labour every three years and your department has been taking exceptional approvals for Gangu. This made him work with us for 15 years, secondly you are paying him more than Rs.16,000/-. If I replace him with other unskilled labour, it will cost you a min pay of Rs.4000/-. Therefore you are actually wasting company funds by paying 8000 extra for a job of loading vehicles. Therefore you will have to put an end to Gangu's contract and that will lead to bigger disturbances because he has now become an integral part of the system. If you renew his contract, we will consider you as a non-complying manager. Therefore, Mr. Ravi, all the best and let me know your decision soon" Shree had a wicked smile on his face.

From the grill, into the frying pan, was Ravi's situation. The first thing that came to his mind was about Gangu's family who was comfortable and would have to go back to 1/3rd the income after 3 months. His second problem was to convince his supervisor and officers closely related to Gangu. In case he does not take a strong decision and renews Gangu's contract, his managerial status would get stained and would also stop his next promotion. He came back to his office and jumped into the HR manual. "What a day!" thought Ravi, "in the morning the battle was in the field and by evening, it had changed to a battle between his heart and his mind."

Sacking the local favourite employee was never an easy job. It becomes still more difficult if you have no other option. Ravi was disturbed. He could no longer focus on work. The event job was suffering. Files were getting piled up with no action. He called his staff and delegated pending work to them. He then just pushed himself out of the office with a question mark in his head.

As he drove back home from work, he looked at the slums where people lived and children played on the road. Scanty clothes, scrap food and hand–to-mouth jobs, but they all appeared happy. Children were laughing and enjoying a game playing using a rotten car tyre. He suddenly realised that happiness was related to expectations and not to income. By the time his car reached home, the decision had been taken. Gangu would have to leave and he would take the bull by the horns.

Gangu also returned home an unhappy man with the union having clearly informed him that they would not be able to support his complaint. The revenge on Ravi sir appeared to be very difficult. He was thinking about turning the tables on Ravi. It was the first night when Gangu was unable to sleep. He also suffered the same state with a tired body and worried mind.

"But why are you not part of the Union?" asked his wife. He did not answer this question. All these years, he had never felt the need to enter the company pay role. The supervisor was happy with him and the salary was increasing. But Gangu forgot that he was doing the same thing all these years and never thought about increasing his role.

The Monday morning department meeting held a very sad silence. Ravi had just made an announcement that Gangu would have to discontinue after the end of this contract and they would have to look out for replacements. After a few minutes of silence, came the arrows "this is what you get for 15 years of service?, is this the way you reward top performers?, how will he survive? his family will go hungry? how can we watch our friend rot? will the same thing happen to us? should we all look for jobs? are they thinking of closing our department?" The arrows were sharp and continued to rain for a few minutes.

Then the judgments followed, "Work will suffer, we will not be able to complete the dispatches in time and spoil our performance, the new guy will never understand our work, the truck drivers will get unhappy, Gangu's family will curse us, the management always harasses non-sales functions, no action is taken on non-performing salesmen, we are not respected, service functions are not important, at this age Gangu will not get a job, his family will go hungry," and many more followed.

Finally it was time for Ravi to speak and he began in a polite but firm tone "Friends! change is the only permanent thing in life. In the corporate world, any person who does not improve, upgrade or educate himself will remain behind, if you are doing the same job, with no additions, at the same designation for more than 10 years, you would certainly come under the scanner, this is the rule of the corporate world. Gangu certainly did a good job for 15 years and got paid higher than industry standards. But he never learned any other activity than lifting boxes and loading them into a truck. He could not even make a photocopy or scan a document. He never made efforts to upgrade his skills and just kept thinking that the world around him will change and keep accepting him. Therefore, the inevitable happened. This is nothing to do with my argument with him. Trust me friends, I ensure you that work will not suffer. At the amount we were spending today, two loaders can be hired for the same job."

He looked at the warehouse supervisor who agreed with the fact that with Gangu's pay, he could hire two workers and double the speed of work.

Eventually the department had to accept the new decision. Gangu was devastated. He had fallen from a peak to ground-level. He moved out before his contract ended. They hired another young worker who was in dire need of the job and delivered with the same efficiency. The HR head appreciated Ravi's decision and gave a high rating to Ravi as well as his boss for selecting the right employee for the organizational talent pool. The next few days, the department was happy because work did not suffer, Ravi's boss was happy, Ravi was satisfied with his decision and HR completed their goals by reducing manpower cost. The exhibition came to an end and the office returned to its normal routine.

"I have a personal demand which you need to satisfy if you want to continue with us, said Ravi to the manpower staffing contractor." He was shocked to hear such a statement because Ravi was not a corrupt man. The supervisor who was seated in the same meeting was also shocked to see Ravi sir openly making such demands. He knew that Ravi was an honest man and such words were very disturbing.

"OK sir," said the contractor "What is your demand? What is it that you want me to do, so that your needs are satisfied?"

Ravi stood up from his chair and kept both hands on the table. He looked into the eyes of both the persons seated in front.

"You will ensure that Gangu Yadav will be placed in a good company with a good salary. Unless you satisfy this personal need, you cannot continue to do business with us" said Ravi.

"Yes Boss!" said the contractor and supervisor together.

Notes

3

Story

Somebody is Watching

A villain is a person hated by all. An office villain is one who abuses others, difficult to approach, constantly involved in humiliating and subordinating others. Overall, the office villain may be a bad boss or employee, part of the organisation and could be harmful to development and creativity. Feedback is not accepted, there is strong resistance to change and worst is that the employee feels proud of his negative actions. This employee could be male or female, young or old, slim or fat, of any religion and residing in any part of the country. There is one such person in every office, two or more in some of the more unfortunate ones.

Culture is the key. Developed mature organisations lay strong focus on culture. Rude behaviour is condemned and action taken immediately. The organisations where such a culture does not exist develop it on their own. This is mostly related to the nature of the boss. If the boss is extremely rude, unethical, continuously paranoid and dictatorial, it keeps employees frustrated for long periods. These frustrations are enemies of creativity, productivity and lead to zero quality. It is true that only happy employees can be creative and can think of improving processes; they make customers happy and also keep suppliers constantly keen on working with the organisation.

In many movies, there is a minor and a main villain. Similarly, in the corporate world, corruption is the biggest and main villain. Corruption is mostly incurable and fatality definitely occurs. Why are people corrupt? What makes them sell their honesty and dignity? In my opinion, the problem arises when demand is greater than supply. Economics is a wonderful subject. When demand is greater than supply ends cannot be met; desire grows and there is a need to increase supply. Increase of supply is possible only if demand is considerably low and under control. However, if demands are exorbitant, supply can no longer be stretched and the criminal part of the mind is activated. This criminal mind then starts getting creative and plans a secret route to achieve more supply. Corruption happens in two cases. The first case is where basic needs of the family like food, clothes and education are not properly met, supply is very low and small bits of theft have to be nibbled at to ensure that demands get barely satisfied. The second case is dangerous because it involves greed. The demands could be to buy land, drink lots of alcohol or just simple greed for money.

This is a story of a corrupt person and a lesson to all. Never accept corruption as part of your world. It will only destroy all those directly and indirectly involved.

Ramesh hailed from a poor family but lived in a very rich neighbourhood. His father was a driver and his mother served as a maid, working in several homes. They lived in one of the garages. As a child Ramesh was included by the rich children while they played cricket or football. They sometimes also invited him to their birthday parties. It was the only time he got to eat delicious food and played expensive games. Eventually this reality ripped his heart into pieces and Ramesh realised that he was not entitled to any of those luxuries, games, parties, bicycles etc. He could only watch and feel sad about it. His parents were honest and hard working. They did not compromise on his education. Ramesh was a bright kid and did well even without coaching classes or extra tuitions. The entire colony was surprised when he scored 85% in standard 10th. His parents could not control their joy and distributed sweets to all. The rich families generously showered gifts and offered monetary support to them.

In college, Ramesh saw this pretty girl whom he instantly took a liking to. Before he could approach her, she had made friends with a rich boy who owned a motorcycle and had lots of cash to spend, eating out and on movies. As this is not a romantic novel, we will skip the details and proceed with the story. Ramesh suffered heartbreak and was terribly frustrated. Then he took a decision, a decision which came from deep inside his heart, a decision which was strong and one that could not be changed under any circumstance. Sadly, the decision was to somehow become rich. If he would have decided to become a great man, this story would have been very different. His only aim was to become rich, really rich and super rich. This shift of focus moved his coordinates. He graduated with only a first class and did not have great marks. The family did not have any more funding to allow him to finish his post-graduation.

The driver's network is always super powerful. They are united and have good contacts in the upper circles. It worked well for Ramesh and he was called for an interview for the position of a clerk in the Logistics department of a multinational. Ramesh was intelligent and did not have any problem clearing the entrance as well as interview. Once again happiness returned to the family. Added income meant a lot, especially to the mother who could now afford to skip a few households' jobs as a maid and these were loaded with heavy work. Ramesh should have been happy on getting a decent job in a big company. However his heart nursed only one desire and the starting salary offered did not even come close to his requirement. His father was happy and purchased two formal shirts for him.

The company had hired ten fresh candidates and placed them in various departments. They all attended Induction Training at the HR department. Everybody was happy and excited. The only person who was silent and serious was Ramesh. His mind was continuously thinking of the route that could be opened and would take him towards his dream. The Induction got completed and Ramesh came to his desk. His boss Mr. Shanmugam, was a happy, honest and kind soul. He treated everybody with great respect. The department of Logistics consisted of imports, exports, local transportation, warehousing and purchase. They were a centralized function and responsible for providing these services to the business.

Shanmugam took personal interest in teaching Ramesh. He also made sure that the company sent him to attend training programs in imports, exports, customs, indirect taxes etc. In two years, Ramesh mastered the game. He was good at his work. The boss was happy with his progress and started to give him independent charge over big shipments. Ramesh was proud of his knowledge but still kept a very introverted and non-friendly approach in the department. He did not make many friends and used his lunch-time reading old company files. The business bloomed and the department expanded from a small team of 6 to 20. Within the first three years, Ramesh was promoted from clerk to "Officer – EXIM". The family for the first time vacated the garage and moved into a one bedroom hall kitchen apartment on rent. For his parents, it was a dream come true, but they did not know that this was not even the tip of the iceberg.

"Son, we are really proud of you" said the father "I think the time has come to for you to get married".

"Not so soon, I need to fulfil my dreams" replied Ramesh.

"What dreams, you are doing very well" said the mother.

"This is not the time, just wait," replied Ramesh.

His parents did not pay much attention and decided to give more time to their only son. They were also very happy and proud of his achievements.

In the next six months, Ramesh was offered independent charge of bill verifications. All vendors who submitted their bills to the company came to his desk. He had to check if they were as per the Purchase Order and then had to forward them to the boss for his signature. Shanmugam trusted Ramesh and signed all the bills that came from Ramesh's desk without question. Ramesh was sharp and efficient. He could verify more bills than the erstwhile person who had by then taken retirement. This role was sure to lead him to the position of Assistant Manager very soon because it had greater responsibility. The desire of becoming rich was not only alive, but thriving within Ramesh.

The question of how to get rich kept rotating and revolving in his mind. There was no answer available but the search was continuous. The thought process was in one direction. The focus was on money. Appreciations of good work done could not satisfy Ramesh.

1st January was the day in his life when the New Year and a new chapter was going to begin. The doors to wealth were to open. He had been analysing the bills of a very big vendor, Lalwani and Sons, who were their customs agents. They cleared all sea and air shipments across all ports in India. Ramesh was always suspicious about their billing. He decided to study the bills. By tea break, he was sure that his observation that this vendor had been adding some kind of extra charges in each bill was correct. Customs' bills have many charges such as carting, demurrage, CFS etc. The bills are complicated, increasing probabilities of over-charging. Ramesh had carefully studied about 100 bills. He also checked the charges and found them irrelevant. "This is my next promotion" he thought and before showing these to his boss, called Mr. Lalwani just to double check.

Ramesh wanted to make a check. But it was important to understand if there was any other special work order that he might have missed. There was a probability that those bills were correct and his analysis was not as per the updated instructions.

"Good afternoon, Mr. Lalwani - this is Ramesh speaking, are you free to talk?" . He was very polite on the phone, especially with rich people.

"Of course Mr. Ramesh, I am always free to talk to the most important and intelligent man in the company" said Mr. Lalwani. He was a sweet talker and a professional businessman.

"Sir, I wanted to discuss some discrepancies in your billing. I have your Purchase Order copy with the agreed terms. I have also cross-checked around 100 bills that you have submitted. Each of these bills has some mistakes. All these mistakes are due to amounts that have been overcharged. I just wanted to discuss if my observations are correct" said Ramesh.

"I have no doubts on your work accuracy sir, but I am sure there must be a misunderstanding" said Lalwani "if you could please check and then confirm which bills are wrong then I'll be highly obliged. We deal with a lot of companies and there is a possibility that we might have made some mistakes. But I am sure that it must be very small amounts" replied Lalwani.

Ramesh was quick to give some Purchase Order data relevant to the case and proved that the billing was indeed incorrect. His observations were written down in a diary. As he was well prepared, it did not take much time to prove that Lalwani was at fault.

"No, problem Ramesh sir, I will make all the corrections immediately. I will rush to your office right away," said Lalwani.

"No, no, not now" said Ramesh "because if this discussion begins by 5 pm, I will surely miss my company bus and will have to walk 2 kms till the public bus stand"

"Why do you need to take the company bus Ramesh sir?" asked Lalwani

"Well, because I do not have any other source to commute. If I had a bike, then I would have definitely waited for you today" said Ramesh.

Lalwani was a very intelligent old man. His listening and superquick analytical skills had given him great success in business. He was seasoned to handle such issues. This was not the first time for him. Lalwani did business with many companies and had a good hold over the right employees.

"OK, Ramesh sir, I will come on 7th Jan, till then just keep this matter on hold. By the way, sir, I have a motorcycle which I no longer use and it is lying idle, why don't you keep it? I will have it delivered to your house on 6th Jan" concluded Lalwani.

Ramesh was completely shaken. This is how you feel when you get indications that your dream will now materialize. He had two choices, one, walk up to the boss, show the report, remove Lalwani and get a promotion next year with an increment of Rs.2000 per month. Or, join hands with Lalwani and get decent compensation right away. He came from a family of honest parents and that had made the process of decision-making really tough. Desire is the route of evil and cannot be controlled so easily. Family values and all the good practices are reinforced in your upbringing, which in Ramesh's case was miserable because he had always been deprived of the good things that his friends so easily obtained.

That evening Ramesh was completely lost. He did not finish his dinner. He was no longer hungry.

"Are you okay?" his mother asked.

"I am all right, just a little tired" said Ramesh.

"Oh my poor boy, he works so hard" said the mother "please have some milk"

"No, I am alright, just feeling sleepy," said Ramesh.

But Ramesh was unable to sleep the whole night. Lalwani's words were biting into his brain. A bike, a vehicle of his own, it was a real big thing for his entire family who did not own anything besides being able to secure two square meals a day.

Probably it was no harm in taking Lalwani's old used bike, thought Ramesh. Nobody will mind an old bike. It will be okay to say yes. His mind was turning very slowly.

On 6th January, Sunday, he realised that Lalwani was lying about the motorcycle he does not use. A brand new Yamaha was standing at his doorstep, with Lalwani holding the key and the warranty card, carrying the delivery-date: 5th January. The bike was a beauty. It was beautiful enough to put a broad smile on Ramesh's face, a smile that had appeared after almost 20 years. He took the key, thanked Lalwani and came home.

"Mom, Dad, I have a surprise for you" said Ramesh.

"Wow, I can't believe it" said his father, while the mother just wiped a tear from her eyes.

They were delighted to see the bike. Parents are keen to see the child succeed. They do not let logic interfere in their enjoyment. The bike was fast, powerful and so was Ramesh. He cleared each and every one of Lalwani's bills with Lalwani becoming his best friend. Ramesh's new chapter in his life's story had just begun to be written.

The world of corruption is perfect. It is very well-organised, planned and all members offer terrific cooperation to all those who they operate with. They are truly devoted to crime and continuously focus on its safety and growth. Lalwani had a bigger circuit of friends and the news of Ramesh was shared in detail in this particular circle. The team understood that the fort held by Shanmugam had been penetrated into with Ramesh's betrayal. This company had now developed a secret passage, where the enemy could enter and sneak in to grab bounties in small quantities in the beginning and huge amounts later.

Yadav Seth was the transporter, who was next to call Ramesh. He was from the Lalwani gang of companies who knew unethical ways of getting more profits.

"Respected Rameshji, please accept our greetings" it was Yadav on the line "I request an appointment with you."

"Yes Mr. Yadav, please come to my office tomorrow," said Ramesh.

His request was that Ramesh should get his bike refuelled at his brother's petrol pump. It was understood that there would be no need to make any payment. When Yadav increased his rate, Shanmugam was the first to object. However Ramesh produced comparative documentation of what others (like him) had paid. He convinced Shanmugam that the price increase was obvious due to the shortage of good transporters in the market. He also certified Yadav for having vehicles following pollution norms. Convincing Shanmugam was not easy but Ramesh had managed it well.

"Petrol is not the only expense I have Mr. Yadav," said Ramesh "the effort required was much more."

"No problem Rameshji sir, your telephone, electricity, water, rent, etc. all bills will be taken care of by our company. You will not have any problem at all" informed Yadav.

Ramesh was now in business. He had taken the reins of the devil's horse in his own hands. Now there was no looking back for Ramesh.

"Mom, you will stop all work, Dad you will now quit your job" he said over the dinner table "I am a consultant to some uneducated petty businessmen and have developed a source of extra income."

"When did you start this business?" asked his father.

"I am doing it along with office work" replied Ramesh "I may have to wait after office hours."

This was the statement for which both of them were waiting for their lifetime.

"Son, you have made us proud and it is now time for you to get married" said the father.

"Do you have any proposal in mind, do you like someone?" enquired the mother.

"No" said Ramesh "I know you wish to have a simple daughter-in-law who would be from our village and caste. Please proceed and I will marry the first girl you select for me."

"Are you sure?" the father wanted to double check.

"Wow!" thought the parents, it was a dream come true. They congratulated themselves for the great upbringing of Ramesh. The matchmaking process began. They informed their friends and close associates. With above-average academic results, Ramesh was already well known in their social circle. This made the process very easy.

Jyoti was a girl who hailed from a very poor family of the village. Her education was limited to high school. She was an ordinary looking girl, timid, traditional and totally submissive, a complete fit to the expectations of Ramesh. He decided to marry her on their very first meeting. For her family, it was the best proposal with no dowry, no demands, good in-laws, an urban lifestyle and a well-qualified son-in-law working at a good position in a foreign company. The wedding was not quite lavish, but some of the gifts were certainly very expensive. This time, all that glittered was gold. It raised questions in the mind of the father however the mother cooled him down with her maternal powers. While signing the documents for the marriage registration certificate, the good wife and obedient daughter-in-law also signed the papers as a director of the Lalwani group. The honeymoon had just begun and it was certainly going to be a long one.

Jyoti was now a business director, a very unique one. A director with no clue about her appointment. She also had an account which was jointly operated with her husband. Money started pouring into this account.

"Have you seen the wedding gifts?" he asked Ramesh.

"Yes, my clients are very rich, they can surely afford them, " replied Ramesh.

With the father raising questions over the gifts, Ramesh understood that the risk of exposure was high because Shanmugam was an honest man. The slightest doubt and he would take action against Ramesh as well as the vendors. This fear was evident with both Lalwani and Yadav, who had now increased costs, with Ramesh becoming an additional expenditure. The option of converting Shanmugam was impossible. Hence it was essential that he would have to be fully eliminated from the scene. Shanmugam had two more years left to retire, but team-Ramesh was not sure of playing the game of hide and seek for 24 months. The risk was simply too high and they were not sure if the new boss also would be honest. Logically it would be the best to remove Shanmugam and place Ramesh as the boss. The three wise men had a meeting in the local bar after office hours. Whiskey flowed like water and a plot was hatched.

Shanmugam was the India head reporting to the global head. Albert headed the global operations. Albert was a serious and very strict type of a person. He visited each country where the company had an office. He did not like people who smiled or laughed or cracked jokes in meetings. It's a strange world. We always believe that serious behaviour is mature behaviour and jovial behaviour displays immaturity. In my personal opinion, maturity is displayed in decision making, employee motivation and the ability to successfully complete a given task. I have observed many serious people taking immature decisions.

Albert did not like Shanmugam at all. This had nothing to do with performances because his operations were almost flawless. His team was happy and motivated. Shanmugam was a fun loving person. He believed that a happy employee will make lesser mistakes and be more productive. He would laugh aloud when somebody made a mistake. His style was effective. The person who made a mistake usually perceived laughter like a slap on the face. Employees then felt bad about themselves and made improvements in their work on their own.

Albert had plans to visit India in June. On announcing Albert's visit, Ramesh went up to Shanmugam and requested if he could coordinate the complete visit. The suggestion was immediately accepted. Lalwani and Yadav had issued special instructions to Ramesh. A complete visit program schedule was well chalked out for the big boss. There were multiple meetings, visits, breaks, lunches, business diners at special restaurants, all well planned and calculated. Pick up time, taxi drivers' telephone numbers, email confirmations of the people attending the meetings, domestic flight bookings, selection of non-veg meals on flights etc., all well set.

Albert was suitably impressed and expressed his appreciation directly to Ramesh who was personally present at the airport at 3 am in the morning to receive him.

"Good morning sir" said Ramesh, as he greeted him at the airport "the odd timings are not safe for foreigners, I could not take a chance. This area is not safe at night for foreigners."

The entire week, Ramesh was glued to Albert. He presented statistical reports to Albert for his meetings with the other departments. He also discussed critical points before their meetings. With this support Albert could make a killing and got most tasks done comfortably. Luck favours those who work very hard. In this case, it did support Ramesh very well. Shanmugam's wife was down with dengue and he couldn't attend many meetings with Albert. This added the icing to the cake that had been so carefully and deviously baked by Ramesh and his friends.

During the meeting with vendors, Ramesh was very strong and very tough against Lalwani and Yadav. He presented all the points that needed improvement. He made them agree and accept their faults. Both of them said that it was the first time that they had been pushed so hard. The entire effort was presented in a way to create a case against Shanmugam making him a weak and casual manager. Albert saw a completely new picture of the department with the absence of Shanmugam. He really liked the picture. This was what he had always wanted. On the last day, Albert had dinner with the entire staff. He openly congratulated Ramesh for his excellent work. Other staff members could smell the butter that had been applied to excess by Ramesh during the week. The dinner bill was paid by Albert. The waiter forgot to bring a pen while signing the credit card slip. Ramesh immediately offered his pen for his signature. He was prepared for everything.

After dinner, Ramesh went to drop Albert to the hotel. When Ramesh was in the taxi with Albert, he decided to sow the seeds of his next attack. When they reached the hotel Ramesh got out of the car and shook hands with Albert.

"Thanks for the excellent support Ramesh" said Albert "it was really a good trip for me. Everything was so well organised and I am impressed with your knowledge and performance."

"Sir, I have a fear and wonder if it is appropriate to discuss this with you openly" said Ramesh. He was acting as if he felt awkward in Albert's presence.

"Sure Ramesh, please tell me" said Albert "there is no need to be formal. I am your boss's boss, but I am also a company employee."

"Sir, my boss is a great guy. I really enjoy working with him, but he is sometimes very casual. You know the repercussions of faulty documentation in India, it can lead to disaster," expressed Ramesh.

Albert kept a hand on his shoulder "don't worry young man - we have capable people in the department who will ensure that nothing goes wrong."

"Goodbye sir and have a safe trip" said Ramesh as he waved goodbye to Albert.

When Shanmugam returned to his office, some of his old trustworthy subordinates gave him a full account of the extra efforts taken by Ramesh to reach closer to the big boss. They also mentioned that he was present in almost all meetings to support him. The problem with good people is that they look at others in a good way and feel that the world around them is good. It is certainly important to trust your team members but leaders cannot be blind, they must be able to smell danger before it comes too close. This plot now had three prominent teams. The first was Ramesh and his friends' circle of wolves like Lalwani, Yadav etc., the second was Shanmugam and his trusted old buddies, the third was the rest of the staff that had been freshly recruited. Gossiping had already begun in the Shanmugam group of oldies for they could smell the nexus between Ramesh and the vendors. The danger towards team-Ramesh appeared to be getting closer and closer. It was time to act.

"Let the war begin" announced Lalwani over drinks during the late-night bar meeting with Ramesh. The second phase of the battle was about to begin. Ramesh had now learnt to drink well having got used to expensive alcohol available in the best of bars.

In the office, he now started taking up fights with the oldies directly. Each matter began with arguments and ended in high definition fights with voices rising above standard office decibel levels. Soft-hearted Shanmugam now found it very difficult to control the fights between his old buddies and star performer Ramesh. Nasty emails exchanged over petty issues eventually reached Albert's desk. He initially did not react but when the frequency increased, picked up the phone and approached Shanmugam. Both of them seemed to have a soft corner for Ramesh who was a common denominator in all battles. They decided to have a teleconference with him before concluding.

"Ramesh, we are seeing a lot of friction in the office" said Shanmugam.

"Could you explain to us why you get upset so frequently?" asked Albert.

"Yes sir, it is my fault" said Ramesh "I am actually finding it difficult to handle the inefficiencies of documentation and the slow speed of some of my team mates. I have been spending sleepless nights over these issues. I think it is simply fatigue. Could you please allow me a long vacation so that I can come back fresh and relaxed?"

"Yes, sure, why not" said Shanmugam. Albert also agreed with this decision. The old officers did not understand the reaction from Ramesh. They were expecting more arguments from him.

Both Albert and Shanmugam smiled at their short-lived success. They felt that their superb mentoring skills had effectively made the mentee open up, after having accepted the problem and their solution to it. A one-month paid vacation was immediately sanctioned. The office was at peace again. The oldies felt that it was just like suspending him from work but in a sugar-coated way. Ramesh and Jyoti were to spend the whole of the next month in their native village. It wasn't a vacation but a cool-off time taken before the final attack is to be launched on an enemy.

It was now time for Lalwani and Yadav to do their job. Their friends' circle was huge. They had the right contacts in all government departments. There was a regular soft-funding that took place in each critical junction. As Ramesh moved out, the Lalwani-Yadav team set up the plot. Funding was abruptly stopped.

The machinery lost lubrication and slowed down its responses. Customs shipments were held up for petty reasons, demanding explanations. Local shipments got stuck between state borders. It created a sudden slow-down in materials' movement. The matter skyrocketed when a very critical spare-part shipment was delayed. There was an equipment breakdown needing critical spares. They had to be imported, air freighted and delivered directly to the factory. Lalwani knew it very well and personally messed up the paperwork. This delay rocked the company. The factory manager demanded Shanmugam's resignation. This news created the right atmosphere for Ramesh to return to the office. He took charge of the shipment, clearing it the next day. Ramesh became a hero and Shanmugam had to take the entire blame on his shoulders. Sudden disruptions in operations brought Albert back to India.

The villain's camp was now ready for the kill and already celebrating. One more big reason to celebrate was that Ramesh had just moved into his own house. It was a moment of great pride for his family.

"I have been investing in the equity market and my intelligence has paid off well" explained Ramesh to the entire guest group who had come to attend the housewarming party.

His wife Jyoti had no idea that her bank balance was now ten times the total life-time amount ever earned by her family. Lalwani and Yadav had their profits improving because of the high rates, duplicate billing and additional charges. Their plan had worked well. It was a perfect case of team work, coordination and cooperation between the three. Ramesh informed them about Albert's surprise visit to India. He also mentioned the meetings going on continuously with Shanmugam.

Monday morning was bright and clear. Ramesh reached his office early. He set up a list of activities to be completed. By lunch he had successfully abused three staff members for no fault of theirs. The wind was on his side and he was sure that Albert was to make an announcement soon about handing charge over to him any day. Shanmugam's cabin was a crowded place. Albert was sitting with two finance officers and Shanmugam was no longer in his chair. He was sitting on the couch kept in a remote corner of his cabin. Ramesh went in just to check the temperature of the room.

"Do you require anything sir" he asked.

Shanmugam did not even look up. Albert smiled at him and said that they will call him soon.

"It is over, we have won" he spoke to Lalwani softly on the phone. The same moment the HR head entered the office. Ramesh was jumping with joy. He was right. Within half an hour from the time the HR head had arrived, they summoned him into Shanmugam's cabin.

The HR head is usually called in when matters get really critical. It was probably required because Albert would have to declare on a dismissal. Ramesh was confident, acting normal and was keenly waiting to accept charge of the department.

"Good afternoon Sir" said Ramesh, as he confidently walked into the cabin. An extra chair awaited him. He sat down and smiled at all the persons seated. Shanmugam still had a gloomy face. His chair was empty. Soon it will be mine, thought Ramesh.

"Well, my boy" said Albert "let me come straight to the point. You are fired."

"What, what did you say? I did not hear well sir" Ramesh was puzzled.

"I said, you have been terminated from your services with immediate effect. Please hand over your computer, mobile phone and cupboard keys. You will be relieved immediately" Albert had a very stern voice.

"What, why, I don't understand" said Ramesh "I have been the best performer and have been taking care of the office so well, one month of vacation and the office comes to a grinding halt, what is the meaning of this? Is this some kind of a joke?" Ramesh lost his cool. This was just not right. How had the tables turned so fast? Ramesh was confused.

Shanmugam got up from the couch and kept a hand on his shoulder. "Ramesh, the provisions mentioned in the Appointment Letter give us the authority to terminate your services if we have necessary reasons, let us not make an issue out of this matter" he said very slowly.

"I will not accept this. I will sue you all, report the injustice in the local newspapers, and this is just not done, I simply do not understand," yelled Ramesh.

"Well" said Shanmugam "just for your kind information, we are also stopping the services from Lalwani and Yadav with immediate effect. They will be soon replaced with a multinational company professionally working on the entire supply chain. The contract has already been signed."

Ramesh suddenly sank in his chair, he was silent, he had no words, they hadn't made any mistake, and their plan had been flawless. Then how had information leaked? He was confused and looked up at all of them.

"It is over, Ramesh, we have been keeping a very close watch on you since the past two months" said the HR head "we have checked the accounts of your wife, places that you visited, people whom you met in the bar etc. We have a full report on your actions and you are very lucky that we are terminating you, else you would rot in jail."

He got up and moved out of the cabin. Handed over the assets and proceeded towards the gate. Both Albert and Shanmugam followed him. The termination letter was handed over to him by an HR officer at the gate. It was "the end" for Ramesh to get a job in any company. As both Albert and Shanmugam returned to their office, they called the staff and made the announcement regarding Ramesh, Lalwani and Yadav.

Ramesh arrived home and informed the family that he had quit his job due to an office fight that he could no longer tolerate.

"What happened, what was the fight about?" asked his father

"They accused me of incorrect working methods " replied Ramesh "I don't want to discuss these issues at all."

When the family is less educated, such lies work. He decided to leave the city forever and start a business in his native village. Jyoti was delighted. They purchased some more land with the cash in her account and rented out the new home. This is how his life changed from a smart corporate officer to a local villager taking care of farming and teaching children at the local village school. It was obvious that his partners-in-crime would no longer support him or be friends. Lalwani and Yadav not only lost a big account but also had to give up their last pending bills fearing legal hassles.

The multinational logistics company soon took full charge generated SOPs (standard operating procedures) and business not only came back to normal, but showed significant improvement.

Albert was happy that everything had been taken care of and it was time for him to leave. That evening, as both of them were having dinner, Shanmugam wanted to discuss Ramesh's case again. But Albert was reluctant. Finally as dinner got over, Albert agreed to discuss it with him.

"Sir, I do understand that all the hidden facts surfaced during our secret audit, but the main question still remains. After the excellent work done by Ramesh, how did it strike you that he was the rotten apple, how did it strike you that Ramesh being the main guy was the main villain?" asked Shanmugam.

Albert had a smile on his face, the waiter brought the bill. He offered his credit card and asked Shanmugam to wait a while. The waiter brought the card slip for his signature.

"May I borrow your pen Shanmugam?" asked Albert.

"Sure, sir, here please take my pen" he said. Albert took his pen, signed the bill and gave it back to the waiter. Before returning the pen to Shanmugam, he had a good look at it. It was a simple ball pen costing not more than one hundred rupees. Shanmugam had a strange look on his face.

"You see, Shanmu, the pen does talk a lot about its owner. In this restaurant on that night, when I was planning to promote Ramesh, I had to borrow his pen and the pen that he gave me was of a top global designer brand. I checked the price of the pen and it was more than 3 times the salary we paid Ramesh. It was impossible for him to purchase it or for any person to give it to him as a gift without a valid reason. I understood that Ramesh was up to some mischief and immediately sent instructions to the Vigilance Team to keep a close watch on his activities. Within a few weeks the picture became very clear" explained Albert.

"As they say, the pen is certainly mightier than the sword," smiled Albert, "Goodnight. All the best! See you again!"

Notes

4

Story

The New Dawn

Every product has a life cycle beginning with the launch, continuing toward maturity and finally entering a state of decline. In the case of human beings, things are no different. We all face difficulties in life. The solution lies in the reaction. A problem can be minimized if we react in a positive way. Good and bad things keep happening. Just think that what is happening is due to the wish of the Almighty. It is God's wish and therefore we need to accept it. I could understand this fundamental concept after reading the Bhagwad Geeta. Product Managers make a lot of efforts to ensure that a product remains in a state of growth for the maximum amount of time. They also make changes so that the product can come out of its state of decline and they can cash in on it as much as they can. Make the same efforts to improve your life, is the message I would like to give in this story. When bad things happen, hold on and hang on, because the night is always the darkest just before the sun rises. After all humans are not different from products, because both need development, grooming, value addition and have a strong urge to earn.

Treat yourself as a product, keep adding value, ensure that the price tag is right, be competitive, keep running the race and never say never again.

All work and no play was Jenny's style. As a teenager, she rarely did what other girls did. She was always engrossed in studies. Clothes, handbags, footwear or make-up were not at all on Jenny's agenda. She was a book-worm. Her academics were brilliant. She achieved high scores in school and decided that she was certainly going to become a Chartered Accountant. It was not a surprise to anybody that Jenny cleared the finals in her first attempt and was a topper. During her college days, she bumped into Satish.

"I love you" he said to her when they met for the first time.

"Get lost" she replied walking away from him.

Satish believe in persuasion. He kept following her patiently every day. He had fallen in love. Jenny too liked him but was shocked at his direct approach and decided to stay away from him. Her focus was on her studies. At college, she wanted to be a topper.

Satish was not as intelligent as Jenny. He stayed at the local hostel. He was good looking and by definition tall, dark and handsome. He was a hard worker who believed in himself and wanted to do something big. In three years of college life, he slowly managed to cast the right impression upon her. Eventually she fell in love with Satish and decided to get married to him.

Satish completed graduation and began to pursue an MBA in Finance. Alone in the city, the boy had the courage to fight for survival in the fast lane with a Western ideology flaunting city culture. The city attracted him and going back to his village was certainly not an option. Satish had a farmer's background. His family had large mango plantations besides others. As a young boy, Satish had spent a lot of time with farmers and used to enjoy himself during a swim in the river every day. His father could only read and understand basic mathematics for business transactions while his mother was uneducated. Both of them had seen bad days and had saved just enough for him to study in the city. They desired that Satish should settle down in their village and look after the plantations. His other relatives also were located in the same or other villages nearby.

When he proposed to Jenny, it had been because of love at first sight. After the academic period, both of them dated and their bonds became very strong. The day arrived when both of them had no choice but to inform their respective families about the relationship and their decision to get married. Both families were shocked and upset. They tried their best to convince the two of them to reconsider their decision. But the young love-birds were firm. Satish's family refused to accept a typical city girl who was not of their caste and also practiced a different faith. They were vegetarians and were not going to bestow their blessings on Jenny who loved beef.

It all turned out therefore to be a total Bollywood style marriage where the boy and girl elope to get married in the presence of friends. Life was beautiful. Both of them had got jobs and therefore financially could easily afford a small apartment on rent. Their love-nest wasn't big but comfortably warm and cosy..

With strong academics, Jenny got placed in a multinational. She was a management trainee in the Finance department. The office was big, well furnished, fully air conditioned, had the best coffee-vending machines, three course meals for lunch and a polite culture. Employees travelled by air and stayed only in five star hotels when deputed to other cities. The company often hired expensive trainers for developing employees' skills. They had Saturdays off, so for all employees weekends began on Friday afternoons. Overall, a happy company to work for, Jenny was always into her job and it was relatively simple. It is believed that larger the organisation, lesser the exposure to complexities. This statement is relative and may not be true in all cases. But in Jenny's case, it was completely true. When complexities are less, perfection arrives quickly. Jenny was intelligent and did her job very well.

Satish got selected in a small Indian company trading in commodities. It was a company where each employee did a lot of multitasking and had practically no fixed job descriptions. The office was below average. It was full of old furniture, typical filing racks, low-cost flooring without carpets and peeled-off paint. There was no provision for tea or food. The employees had to manage on their own by eating out at road-side stalls. Work was a six-day week and travel strictly by bus and rail. Air travel and star hotels were not allowed. Air-conditioning was only in the boss's cabin and he earnestly believed that employees couldn't work if they are not yelled at or continuously harassed. Training or employee development was never on the agenda. The culture was rough, language was rougher and warmth did not exist. The job was tough, complex and the measly rewards were strictly result-oriented. If results weren't achieved, the boss would shake you out of your orientations with sadistic pleasure.

We join a company to work, learn, make a living and build a career. But lot of importance is given to facilities and infrastructure that an organization provides. Employees forget to see what they are learning, how much they are contributing and just focus on what extra items the coffee vending machine delivers. Tomato soup, chicken soup, hot chocolate, along with four types of coffees and different kinds of tea become the main motivators to go to work. Employees actually check if five star stays are permitted before saying 'yes' to a new job or sometimes switch jobs only because their current company does not provide the same. There was a case where an employee quit a semi-government job because they allowed her to fly only

Air-India and she could not experience the luxuries of other airlines. I am not saying that such facilities are not needed or aren't important. Yes, they certainly boost the employees' morale and make them happy. It is proven that happy employees can make customers happy. Creativity, out of the box thinking, process improvement and complex problem-solving can be done better by happy employees. It all depends upon who you want to be in an organisation and the height to which you desire to climb. If ambition isn't high and a stress-free life is an objective, then job description, learning opportunities and mental values will not get priority. When you are gunning for the most important chair, then such frills have to be considered secondary. The entire focus should be on the job description, exposure, challenges and people-management opportunities that your current employment has on offer.

So Jenny and Satish both experienced contrastingly different environments at work. Usually a talkative partner discloses all that happens at work in minute details. In our case Jenny was the talkative one. She used to express her happiness at the luxuries provided in her office with Satish who sadly had nothing much to talk considering what he was going through. He used to silently listen to her elaborate stories about conferences in five-star hotels, the gigantic platters of food in the buffet, the rooms' ambience full of grandeur etc. Satish was strong and could take hardships at the office and still continue to learn, work and deliver good results. There was no complaint from his boss who performed well because of Satish. Jenny too, being sincere, did her work honestly.

A year went by and the overall situation continued to remain the same. Then suddenly life took a nasty turn with Jenny getting a new boss. He was an Indian born and brought up in America. He liked Jenny for various reasons but more because she was attractive. He wouldn't leave a single opportunity to have any kind of interaction with her. These slowly advanced at a rapid speed, eventually becoming physical and unpleasant. It began with a simple hand-shake or just a pat on the back. As days passed by, the touch progressed to her arms and shoulders. Jenny was terribly uncomfortable. She lost focus. . Every morning he would spend time at her desk. He would have coffee with her. Lunch was always together. She did try to slip out or hang out with other lady colleaagues in the department but he kept moving closer. Somehow she couldn't share this discomfort with Satish who was already tense because of his work. Jenny had painted such a rosy picture of her office and surroundings that this new sexually hateful and dark episode had to be swept under the carpet. It is very unfortunate that there are so many employees who silently bear discomfort at the workplace for various reasons.

Satish got to assume more responsibilities. He also became popular because he was the only employee who could handle the boss's fury. This took a toll on him. Work-related stress usually comes uninvited and disturbs a person. For our couple the stress had enveloped them comprehensively and both of them were unaware of the partner's deep distress. Each thought that it was okay to be in stress as long as the partner was comfortable and doing well in the office. This thought increased expectations and as we all know, expectations often lead to sorrow.

Thus began the next chapter full of arguments, fights, yelling at each other, abusing each other's families, loss of romance etc. For Satish it was too much work at the office, a bad boss, employees with no motivation, unhygienic office conditions and a stressed-out wife when she returned home. For Jenny, it was a golden-cage of an office, harassment by her boss and a tired and frustrated husband at home. Dinner time was uncomfortable, with fights continuing even at the breakfast-table. The neighbours heard noises and were entertained by the couple's squabbling.

Eventually, the volcano erupted. Two slaps, almost together. The first came from Satish on Jenny's face and the second from Jenny on her boss's face. The honeymoon, long over had now made even terminated the marriage and Jenny resigned. The landlord was given a month's notice. Both vacated the flat, going back to their pre-marital homes. Satish too resigned before moving back to his village. It was a sad moment but they refused to budge with each one's ego coming in the way.

A chapter came to an end fot Jenny and Satish. The marriage was over. The predictions of their parents had come true with both of them having realized that life wouldn't ever be the same again.

The staff in Jenny's office staff couldn't accept the fact that her resignation had no reason. They thought that probably it was her marriage that had suddenly gone bad. She never declared or discussed what had happened with her due to taboos and embarrassment ensuing. She had slapped the boss in his private and enclosed cabin therefore nobody knew that such an incident had actually occurred. The boss was happy to accept her resignation and relieved her instantly. He was actually elated for his crime had gone unpunished. Most harassment crimes in our country are swept under the carpet.

She went back home and wept almost three days running before returning to normal. Her parents supported her and she started looking for a new job. Web portals, newspapers, consultants and friends, she did not leave a single stone unturned. Most of the positions did not accept her application because of her high salary expectations. Certain companies do not hire those who are at present unemployed. Overall it is really difficult to land a job when you're jobless. One must swallow frustrations and look out for a job before throwing that resignation into the boss's face. A company shortlisted her and called her for an interview. She entered the office and saw it far below her expectations because the housekeeping was terrible, the toilets were stinking and members of the staff were shabbily dressed. She waited at the reception for her interview. After two hours, she was called inside.

"Why did you quit the job you were doing?" was his first question.

She stumbled a little and said "Well, sir, I wasn't comfortable and had to resign."

"What do you mean by 'not comfortable'?" was his second question. "Was there any problem?"

"I would prefer not discussing the matter sir, I hope you understand," replied Jenny. She was not going to open up, "I would not be in a position to discuss further," was her direct response. The interviewer suspected some kind of a fraud or mistakes or maybe even a petty crime for it appeared obvious.

"I just wanted to know why you left the last job. It is very important for us. Who was your last boss? Is it possible to contact him for reference?" he asked. There was a long pause after this question. Jenny did not know what to say. Her boss was not going to tell the truth and his lies would put her in more trouble.

"Thank you sir and have a nice day" was her reply.

"What, what do you mean madam? Have I said something to upset you?" the interviewer was surprised.

She got up and left the office without looking behind. Something was not right. She was no longer the same. Life was a blank. No job, no Satish, no house of her own and an empty mind. A situation perfect for creating an invitation to depression.

Satish was sitting under a tree. That is what he did all day after coming back to the village. He deeply regretted what he'd done. It was not right to have slapped her, he thought, the guilt consuming his conscience. But the courage to go back and say "sorry" was missing. His old parents unable to understand, were deeply concerned about him.

"It is okay, life will come back to normal" his mother consoled him every day. But Satish was definitely depressed..

His friends from the village had all settled down in their family businesses or had gone abroad to work. The village was no longer the same again. Life was a long silence. The only noise came from the wind that made the leaves talk. They were all saying that he was completely wrong. There was no solution. He could not change what had happened. He also realised that she was far superior to him in many aspects. She was more intelligent, had a better job and a great career ahead. He thought that there was no point in spoiling her life. She would certainly not fit into a marital situation with a person who is below-average. He was really low and passed a few more days with lunch and dinner being eaten, sitting under the tree.

"You are a professional, a well-qualified professional, why don't you start your own practice?" asked Jenny's father, who was upset at seeing his daughter in this state.

There was no answer; she was entering the first stage of depression. He was really worried and spoke to some of his business friends to hire her. He requested them to take second opinions from her as a free-of-cost service. It was obvious that she would become normal only if she had work in hand. Two of her father's business friends agreed and Jenny started visiting their offices to conduct audits. Both the offices were exactly the same - small, poor infrastructure and practically no facilities for the employees. Just like his office, she thought about Satish, a tear rolling down. She now understood how he would have felt when she used to continuously boast about her bigger office and its facilities. You come to know a person only when you step into his shoes, so true, thought Jenny. She was able to relate to how he patiently kept listening to her stories of luxuries that had been denied him. His frustrations might have made him raise his hand she thought, It was my fault, she told herself, but perhaps it was a bit late.

It was harvest time back in Satish's village. The villagers were excited. The crop had been good. They were expecting to make decent money. Everybody except Satish was in a celebratory mood..

"We are dealing with our buyers today and you will attend this discussion" said his father.

"No, I don't feel like going anywhere" replied Satish.

Satish was really not interested. But his father wasn't ready to accept Satish's decision to stay back home and sit under a tree. It was his mother who emotionally pushed him out to accompany his father in the business deal.

"You will go with your father. Son, please don't make me cry!" his mother was already crying while speaking those words. Satish was not able to see his mother in tears. He knew that she would cry the whole day and therefore decided that it was a better option to go out with his father and attend the buyer's meeting.

The fat buyer had come from the city. He arrived in a Mercedes, had three smart phones and a secretary who looked more like his bodyguard. The other plantation owners were also present in the room. Tea was ordered for all. They greeted the fat buyer by bowing with folded hands. He was being treated like a maharajah. A table fan was kept pointing directly at his couch along with a bottle of cold mineral water. The buyer was arrogant. He started speaking in a strange tone. His words and his style of delivering them were such that it appeared as if he was doing the villagers a big big favour.

"The market is very weak, but I will still ensure that your hard work is taken care of" he said patronizingly.

Satish was more interested in the tea that had been prepared with special spices. He was not going to interfere in the discussions. As the fat buyer announced the purchase price, the villagers became happy. He also declared that the payment would be made upfront - and in cash. The sellers were overjoyed. They praised the buyer and once again bowed with their hands folded.

"What a stupid buyer," thought Satish, "he is paying them the same price prevailing in the city." Then he was a little surprised, because the cost of transportation would certainly play a major role. Therefore it was impossible for the buyer to make a profit instead he would surely be undergoing a loss. "Why is this fellow willing to undergo a loss?" thought Satish, "Is he planning to use the shipment to hide drugs?" He came out of the room and asked one of the buyers:

"Hey brother, how come the buyer is offering such a high price per piece?" he asked.

The fellow had a big laugh "have you lost your senses in the city?, the price is for a dozen and not for a single piece," he replied.

"What?" yelled Satish, "are you all idiots, this guy is conning you!"

Some of the villagers came out to see why Satish was talking in such a loud voice. They asked him to lower his voice. But Satish wasn't going to listen to anybody. He kept his tea-cup down and walked into the meeting.

"This rate is not acceptable" he spoke straight to the fat buyer.

"What do you know about this business?" asked the buyer.

"Just shut up and sit outside!" said his father.

All the other villagers were upset with Satish. They were amazed to see Satish talking so loudly for the first time.

"Just try to do it yourself and then you will understand how much is the cost to take them to the main market, how much we have to pay the local authorities, the police, the local goons," the buyer was speaking in an agitated tone, "I am taking so much trouble trying to manage all kinds of uncertainties, who do you think is going to take care if the fruit is damaged in transit?"

The unscrupulous buyer, appearing angry spoke at length. He was not looking at Satish and was addressing the villagers.

"Young man, better leave this room, before I decide to go without making a deal," said the fat buyer.

The other villagers agreed with him and Satish was asked to leave the room.

"Okay, I will not sell my fruit to you!" said Satish and walked out of the room.

"Get lost, I don't care!" said the fat buyer.

"Please excuse my son, he is very depressed. Please accept my apologies for his rude behaviour!" Satish's father was almost on his knees.

The buyer had the strength of numbers; he took it as an insult and refused to accept the fruit from Satish's father. The other villagers sympathized with him. They quietly signed the document and walked out of the room. The fat buyer gave instructions to his secretary. He went straight to the Mercedes that had its engine running for the air conditioning to work. There was gossip amongst the villagers, they all felt that Satish should apologize to the buyer. There was no point in making him upset at this stage. What would happen when in the next season he didn't return? The thought itself was scary. They decided to speak to Satish's father that night.

"Satish has ruined my business" shouted his father as he entered the house.

The mother was now crying loudly. She was highly emotional. Satish was their only son.

"Something is terribly wrong with our son. Some evil spirit has cast a spell on him. I will pray to God and fast for his life" she said sobbing bitterly.

Some of the villagers gathered at their house that night. They had a discussion on how the situation could be improved. Satish was not at home. He was upset by the manner in which the villagers were being cheated. He decided to fight and help them. Information Technology would make it easy for him to sell their produce without middle-men making a fortune out of the hard work of the villagers.

Jenny's audit was a disaster. She pointed out innumerable flaws. Stocks had been manipulated, the sales figures were 20% lower than actual and evasion of taxes was rampant. Overall she concluded that this business was not being conducted in a fair manner. It came as a big surprise when the owner of the business acknowledged and accepted the non-compliances that she reported.

"Welcome to the world of small businesses" he said while laughing at her, "to be competitive and survive, it is very important that such minor maladjustments be accepted."

"Yes sir, but it is wrong and how will you manage the assessments?" asked Jenny.

"Don't worry dear, that part is fortunately easy to manage," he had a broad smile on his face.

"Sorry sir, I don't do things that are not true and fair, thank you and all the best" Jenny had by now become used to walking out of offices.

Back home, Jenny's father was not happy. His daughter had spoiled the relations he had built over the years with his friends. His friend called and complained "Your daughter is egoistic and rigid, please do not send her to my office again if you want our friendship to continue," he was quite firm..

Her mother was upset. She was unable to see her daughter depressed. She regularly spoke to her sister who was flourishing in Goa. Each discussion began with Jenny and ended up in Jenny's mother sobbing on the phone. Both the sisters seemed to get satisfaction after this emotional release.

It was Jenny's aunt in Goa who advised that Jenny should permanently get out of Mumbai, which was probably not letting her forget Satish and come to Goa.

"She can live with me and help in my business" she insisted.

Her aunt had liked Jenny since her childhood. But Jenny was too down and did not want to mess up her only aunt's business. Jenny thought of herself as a total failure, "life would never be the same again after the many mistakes that I have made," her thoughts were sad.

"Good morning sir, I have an appointment with your general manager – Purchase" said Satish to the good looking receptionist. He had arrived in the city office of a very large retail chain.

"Please take a seat," she said.

It was exactly two hours of waiting before she called out his name. He entered the cabin and sat in front of the General Manager. Satish was fully prepared with the photographs, samples and copies of documents etc.

"We have an annual rate contract with Mr. Harkisandas, he ensures that we get a continuous and single point supply for the entire season, it is not possible for us to deal with multiple farmers," the general manager was direct and steady with his words, "Thanks for your visit." Harkisandas was the very same fat buyer who had come to his village.

He then visited a distributor who had the same story to tell. Another mall chain again had Harkisandas already present. His hands were longer than his Mercedes. Satish was staying with a friend and called home that night. Before he could speak to his mother, his father had put the phone down. Satish was really upset.

"He had called, he knows that you are trying to approach the market directly" said his father "he was very upset."

"What are you talking?" asked Satish.

Harkisandas had called his residence; his sources had informed him that Satish was making an attempt in the market. Which means that his father would have to struggle much more now and if required even give his produce to Harkisandas without charging a single rupee. Next day at the wholesalers' fruit market, Satish understood that they all had a fixed chain that was virtually impossible to be broken. His stepping in to help had been a miserable failure. He had pulled the trigger without thinking of the consequences. He realised that it was probably a bigger mistake than slapping Jenny. The next problem was to go home and face his father as well as the villagers who had now developed a grudge against him. They would probably request him to leave the village. "What have I done?" thought Satish as he walked along the road. He was actually walking without even knowing where he was headed. He had nowhere to go. A few minutes later, he was tired. But he still kept walking till he was about to faint. The sun was shining, it was hot and humid. As he looked towards the other side of the road, he saw a church.

It was a big church and had a large row of seats. He stood at the door of the almost empty church. He did not have the courage to walk in further and sat down in the last row. His mind was blank. He was staring at the candles when he remembered a pleasant incident in the church with Jenny. Tears started rolling down his eyes. The priest came from behind and kept a hand on his shoulder.

"What is the problem my son?" he asked. Satish could not speak. He just sat down in tears. The priest sat beside him.

"Tell me son, this is the house of God, He is listening to you" said Father.

"I am a loser, Father" said Satish "a big and all-round loser"

"No, son, nobody is a loser, it is all about circumstances" said Father, but Satish interrupted him.

"I have destroyed my marriage, I have messed up my father's lifetime's business, I have put an end to my career, I have nowhere to go," said Satish. He was totally down.

"Don't worry my child, God will make everything okay" said Father.

"No Father, nothing can be done now, I will just have to struggle with my life all alone. Search for an accommodation, search for a job, I just don't know where to go" said Satish.

"I messed up my marriage, gave sorrow to my wife, my parents, it will not be easy to get a job. What can I do now?" Satish was in tears.

"It is really a strange coincidence. I have just now come across a similar story from that girl seated in the first row. Let me introduce both of you, sharing a problem might make the two of you feel a little better," He took Satish and dragged him to the first row.

She was sitting with her head buried in her hands.

"Jenny my child, say hello to a new friend" said Father.

As she turned her head, bells started ringing. Yes, it was she. Satish was delighted to see her. It was his Jenny. She looked at Satish and jumped into his arms.

"I am sorry," said both of them simultaneously, "No, I am sorry" said both again at the same time.

Father appeared surprised. He was glad to see both of them coming out of their sorrow.

"This is my husband, Father" said Jenny "It is indeed a miracle, I was just thinking about him"

"God is great" said Father and left both of them to settle down. They cried, hugged and kissed. It was like a big load off their chest. It was a feeling of relaxation, a joy that was so sudden, so unexpected that they took time to get normal again.

At the coffee shop, Jenny told him about the harassment at work, other offices that she had been to and Satish recounted his story about the village and business problems. They both confessed their mistakes. Grief is inversely proportional to a fighting spirit. With the sudden letting go of grief, they were again able to stand up and fight. The power that had brought them together would now also grant them the power to fight the world together.

"If you are with me, I can fight ten villains like Harkisandas" said Satish. Jenny laughed aloud. It was her first laughter after a long time.

She reached home and jumped in joy when she informed her parents that she had patched up with Satish. This time, it was her parents who had wet eyes. A child's happiness is the biggest joy for any parent. They were glad that Jenny had come out of her depression and was dancing again. They asked her to bring Satish home and decided to let go of all caste differences. Satish was also happy to hear that Jenny's parents had accepted their marriage. He moved out of his friend's house and moved in with them for an emotional union.

What now? This was a question now uppermost on their mind. Going back to the village was a no-no for Satish because the entire group of villagers and his father too were against him. Staying at Jenny's house was also not a comfortable option. Searching for a job was not easy because his last office was not going to give him a clean chit for quitting suddenly without any reason. His boss certainly was not an angel to accept his apologies and take him back. Jenny was happy to have Satish back - her financial situation was just about okay to sustain them for a year, as she had some good FDs untouched. Her parents were happy to see their daughter come out of depression and were ready to accept whatever decision they took.

"Send both of them to Goa" said Jenny's aunt over the phone.

It was Jenny's aunt's decision that they should both come to her place and help with her distribution business. Both Satish and Jenny did not have an option, but a trip to Goa would be relaxing and a good change from the current city. They boarded the train to find out what destiny had in store for them.

Jenny's aunt was a hardworking woman. She and her husband ran a distribution business. They collected multiple products manufactured by large, medium and small sized companies. These products were stocked in their warehouses and distributed to a large chain of retailers all over the state. They had a network of delivery vehicles, drivers and workers. Every day they would speak to the retailers and collect orders. These orders were piled on pre-decided routes, picked from their warehouse and delivered the next day before customers arrived in the shops. They operated on very low margins but kept service-levels extremely high. Shopkeepers were happy with their services. Both husband and wife worked very hard. Coordination, planning, manpower management, vendor management was done meticulously. They had no children and treated Jenny like a daughter.

Jenny and Satish reached Goa on a Sunday. They had some time to relax and enjoy the evening on the beach before getting to work. Monday morning was a busy day for aunty. She was taking Satish and Jenny around the warehouse. Her office assistant gave her the delivery report. It was not good. She was worried because one of her manufacturers continuously failed to deliver on time. "These home grown businesses are so unprofessional," she was telling them, "They could beat the big brands easily just by becoming organised and systematic," she insisted.

"What products are we talking about aunty?" asked Satish.

"My dear boy, these are a group of women who make pickles, jams, preserves etc. there is a big demand for these products but we have to simply depend on the big brands who deliver low quality products at higher prices to us" she replied.

Satish suddenly jumped up from his chair. "I can do this" he said.

"What are you talking about?" asked Jenny.

He sat down and looked at Jenny's aunt. "How many orders can you give me for pickles, jams and other products made of mango, jackfruit, papaya and banana?" was his question.

"If the taste and service is good, we can sell a very large quantity in retail and if you package them well, then the entire Goa hotel industry will be our customer" she replied.

"I will produce them for you at my village and be your supplier" said Satish confidently.

The next two days, Satish spent a lot of time studying the products, their packaging size, the distributor's landing price, the MRPs, the brand design, the variety that sold more than others, etc. He prepared a quick report on his study and compared various costs. Jenny wasn't too happy about the idea of becoming a rural manufacturer. She was also worried about being accepted by his family. But Satish was determined, he wanted to convert his village into a manufacturing base and stop bowing to fat middlemen who were exploiting them. However the problem was the initial investment. He would need money to buy the packs, infrastructure, pay salaries, buy raw material. This was a tough task. Jenny was determined not to take further help from her aunt or parents, but she wanted to see Satish succeed in any case. The decision was taken to use all her remaining fixed deposits as well as her jewellery. But the investment was still not enough. Her aunt was aware of their plans. She offered to buy their entire lot in an unpacked condition. She was planning to repack the goods in her own premises, under her own brand. This would help her become a semi-manufacturer and diversify from the core business of distribution. Satish was not in agreement with this proposal, but he had no choice.

Satish would need more than his own production to complete Jenny's aunt's order. He would also need workers and premises. But the biggest hurdle was to face his parents and the villagers. They wouldn't agree with his line of thinking. Harkisandas would have by now created an aura of hate for Satish. Convincing the villagers appeared to be difficult as they had already labeled him a boy who does not understand business and who had messed up the earlier convenient setup with their only buyer. When you decide to fight after a big failure, the brain becomes more agile. Ideas flow in faster than before. Learning from mistakes is one of the best forms of learning.

Satish purchased two suits and hired a taxi with a driver. He entered his village during the Saturday panchayat meeting, when the villagers including his father would be present. The car drove up, right in front of the meeting. The driver got out and gave a look to all the villagers who stopped their discussions and were staring at the car. Then the driver went to the other side of the car and opened the rear left door. Satish emerged, wearing a suit and big sunglasses. At first sight, the villagers could not recognize him at all. As he entered the meeting and removed his sunglasses, they were shocked; "Saatissh!" was their first reaction.

"Namaste to all, greetings dad" said Satish as he went and sat down on one of the chairs. His body language was the same as Harkisandas. The villagers were stunned. They all got up and gathered around Satish.

"I am now a buyer" said Satish as he put a bundle of notes on the table. They all had an expression of awe. He also explained to them his plans of putting up a unit that would make many products. It would not just bring in money for fruit but also provide a source of income for others. Satish was now their official hero.

At home that night, his parents were very happy to have their son back as a businessman.

"How did you manage it?" his father was talking to him for the first time since his return to the village. Satish told them the entire story. They had realised their mistake on having judged Jenny incorrectly and decided to accept her as part of the family.

This story ends as Satish and Jenny come out of their failures, turned a village around into a production hub, became distributors to other places besides Goa and eventually built their own brand. After all, big successes come after big failures.

"You are fired Mr. Sampat" said the Managing Director "this is your termination letter. The Internal Complaints Committee has taken this decision based on the complaint of our ex-employee, Ms. Jenny and a few other female employees."

Three female employees were happily discussing issues during lunch and thanked Jenny for her brave initiative.

"And her pickles are yummy too" said one of them. The remaining nodded in agreement.

Notes

Run Boy, Run…

"Cash or card sir?" asked the cash counter officer at the shopping mall.

"Card", said Neil "I have a credit card"

He was on top of the world. He was flying high and felt great. The purchase included a pair of denims, sunglasses and two shirts. All the items were of premium brands. Neil was a rich boy. Richness is of two types. The first is the really rich and the second is the situational rich. Neil belonged to a middle class family. He lived in a 400 square feet house with six family members, including parents, grandparents and a younger brother. His parents served in different companies and made just enough to make two ends meet and were also able to afford a decent education for their children. Neil was a situation rich. He had just received his first salary in his first job. He did not have many expenses. The house, food etc. were all managed by his parents. His entire income was therefore his to dispose and enjoy. Life was a bed of roses.

At work, he had been appointed as a management trainee. It was through campus placements for fresh MBAs. The company had visited many colleges across India to hire talent. They hired 15 fresh MBAs. However before actually joining, 8 MBAs had got better offers and did not join. Thus, finally only 7 had come on board.

The batch of 7 was surprised to experience the royal treatment they received from the company. They also received a cold shoulder from other employees. The other employees saw this group of seven as a gang and a threat to their own positions. After a few days, the entire batch of recruits was deputed on a six months Induction Program. Under this Program these trainees travelled across locations and departments. They were provided high-end hotels because this was a talent-grooming program with a high budget.

There is a transition phase between college and work-life. College is fun and adventure. College is all about passing examinations and having a great time with friends. Smoking, drinking and partying are regular. This attitude comes with the new trainees. It takes some time for young recruits to emerge out of their college shells. Till then, they try to live a college type lifestyle even at work.

All the 7 wanted to have fun, but two out of them were extra smart. Neil and his buddy Depen were bold, smart extroverts who enjoyed taking risks. They used to sneak out during work. The worker's recreation area was their favourite spot. It had indoor sports like table tennis and carrom. While the other 5 trainees spent their time on the shop floor these two were happy playing carrom.

PP Alloys was a subsidy of a global auto-component manufacturing giant. It produced specialized components for the auto industry. They had set up manufacturing units in Pune and Chennai. The company's headquarters were in Pune. The company hired a batch of fresh MBAs and groomed them to take up senior positions based on their capacity and competence. The company rarely hired employees in a senior position from outside. This was a cost-effective strategy. It also created a good growth path for the employees. Neil was now part of this company. He had been handpicked by Head of Operations, Mr. Patel. Patel was a smart leader. He knew what these two were up to, but wanted them to sever their college ties slowly.

It was a Monday morning. The trainees were taken into the heat treatment department. The head of the department was personally showing them the facilities.

"Carbon and nitrogen are simultaneously introduced into the ferrous alloy by heating while in contact with molten cyanide, followed by quenching to produce a hardened case. Please note that cyanide is dangerously poisonous. You must wash your hands every time you touch the equipment and before you leave the lab," he insistently warned them.

Both Neil and Deepen were not listening. They had been to a disco in Pune till late last night. With lack of sleep, spending time in the heat treatment lab was killing. As the group moved ahead toward the next equipment, both stayed back looking at each other. Carrom seemed to be the obvious choice. Just as they were sneaking out, Patel walked in.

"No, no boys, nobody leaves the cyanide lab without washing their hands," he said.

"Oh sir, we were on our way to the toilet" said Deepen.

"Okay, no worries," he said and walked away. It was an easy escape.

But with an agile leader, you cannot be lucky all the time. Patel knew the trends of young recruits and he kept a watch. They still managed to cheat him a couple of times. The boys were smarter than him most of the time.

Unfortunately, he caught them red handed smoking in the sports room the next day.

He made them wash their hands and then took them into his office. He looked angry. They had realised it was trouble. They had committed two crimes, sneaking away from work and the bigger crime was smoking. The organisation had a very strict No Smoking policy.

"Look, I can understand that you are interested in marketing. I also understand that you are just out of college. But there are things that you have to do. This is an organisation, not a club." He was polite but firm in his words.

Both of them apologized and promised to be serious. It is obvious that they were not serious and were caught sneaking out pnce again. This was a serious offence. Letters were issued giving a final warning. Now playing carrom was restricted to only 15 minutes post-lunch. Smoking was totally banned. It was mental torture for Neil and Deepen.

Intelligent minds are creative. Creativity works in good as well as bad areas. They were continuously thinking of a plan to outsmart Patel. The training at the lab would last more than three weeks. They were not going to accept defeat.

The lab was safety compliant. It had two exits. There was a third exit through the janitor's room. The janitor's room had a long and narrow passage. It was very dusty. With automatic floor cleaning equipment, the janitor's room was no longer being used. This passage connected the heat treatment lab to the janitor's area. Neil and Deepen had discovered a unique place which had almost been forgotten. It was a great place to smoke or just sneak out of the lab into.

The smoking and carrom continued but with caution. The secret passage was used often. The organization also conducted random entry checks to ensure that the employees did not bring cigarettes or other restricted items. Therefore the passage was also a resourceful area to hide cigarettes. There were several empty cupboards in the passage. It was easy to hide practically anything.

Friday evening, Patel conducted a surprise test. It was followed by a serious lecture delivered to Neil and Deepen.

"You guys need to understand that such poor performances will lead to severe consequences" said Patel.

"Sorry sir, we will definitely improve," was the reply. But the boys were still boys.

The evening was full of fun in the local bar. The boys drank with no regrets. Neil was confident of getting his records straight in Sales. Deepen was planning to join his father's business after working here for two years.. Therefore both were comfortable with the hospitality of the organisation, notwithstanding the minor and irritating interactions with Patel. The fresh stocks of cigarettes were smuggled inside, as a new week began. A different cupboard was opened to keep them.

But this time, the cupboard already held some polythene bags. The bags were dust-free, implying that they had been recently added. Somebody was using the passage to store things. It was not secret anymore. This was a sad situation. If the passage was being used for work, then it was obvious that they would get caught.

The boys wanted to understand who was using it. They kept an eye on that area. But for two days, they did not see any one enter or even mention the storage. It was important to know who was using the storage area. Another way to find out more about the user was to check what material was being stored in the bags.

"See what is in the bag," said Deepen

"White coloured candy like big chunky tablets. I remember seeing them somewhere," said Neil.

The clock struck 6 followed by a loud siren. It was time to leave. While washing their hands, Deepen asked the senior technician "Why do we always keep washing our hands sir?"

He took them to a double locked closet, marked with a symbol indicating "Danger" and showed them the poisonous chemical containing cyanide. He also informed them of the strict regulation of washing hands. Death was immediate even if a few molecules were swallowed. This knowledge further confused them. The chemical that had been shown was similar to the one they had seen in the janitor's narrow passage.

"Why are they keeping extra cyanide in our area?" asked Deepen.

"It is not our area stupid," said Neil and they both had a laugh.

The end of the third week brought them to the last day of training in the lab. It was time for them to pick up the remaining cigarettes and look out for a new hiding place. Out of curiosity, they checked the cupboard in which cyanide was stocked.

"It is empty. They have stopped using this storage just as we are leaving," said Deepen.

"Bad luck bro, let us see what opportunities we get in the new department," said Neil.

The Induction Training Program gave them exposure to different departments. They would be spending one or two weeks in each department subject to the importance or complexity of the same. The next department was the shop-floor. It was full of large computer aided machines capable of cutting, shaping and polishing metal components. It was the biggest department in the complex. Each machine was manned by a worker. The work took place in three shifts. For every 4 to 5 machines there was a supervisor and the department had three engineers for the three shifts.

It was a department under the strictest of vigilance where mischief was virtually impossible. The work was physical and the boys were expected to help the workers. It was hands-on learning. The slow process of breaking college kids into real men had begun.

This period was unbearable for both. They used to get tired by the evening and it practically stopped all the good part which was their night life. Somehow they suffered the tough phase by continuously cursing the systems of the company.

Two weeks of hard work had come to an end. The next department was Stores. This could be a relief. The batch was greeted by the Head of Stores. He asked them to go through the manuals. The girl who handed over the manuals was very pretty. Neil could not take his eyes off her.

"Hi, I am Neil," he said to her with a decent smile. She just handed over the manuals to him and did not smile back.

"Thanks Senorita" he said.

"I am Anita" she said, this time with a smile.

Neil was trying to appear cool, but his heart was jumping with joy. Deepen could not understand the sudden burst of radiance in his eyes. It was love at first sight for Neil. Deepen did not believe in it. He just laughed at Neil.

"It is lunch time," said Neil to Anita.

"I know it. I am your senior at work," she replied.

"Could you show me the Stores and guide me?" Neil requested. She did not react.

"Let's have lunch." Neil was an aggressive pursuer.

"I am not from Stores. I am an auditor," she replied.

"I guess auditors also have lunch," he said. She smiled. They went to a corner table. Deepen pushed himself on the same table.

In the next couple of days, the three of them became good friends. Anita was a fresh commerce graduate. She was pursuing higher education to become a Chartered Accountant. She was working for an audit company that had deployed her in PP Alloys.

During one of their lunches, Anita appeared really worried. She was upset and irritated.

"What is bothering you?" asked Neil.

"The safety officer, Ramanuj has been very rude to me," she said.

Both the heroes were charged up, wanting to save her from that villain. On further discussion, they understood that he was accusing her of incorrect stock count of the critical stock.

"Is the stock very expensive?" asked Deepen.

"No, but hazardous and poisonous, the physical stock of cyanide is actually less than what it should have been," she replied.

"Are you talking about the big white pills in the heat treatment lab?" asked Neil.

"Yes, when I checked, the stock was less, but when Ramanuj checked after two days, it was perfect. He accused me of being careless and reporting wrong figures to the management. According to him, I am not capable. He has recommended that I be suspended from PP Alloys," she was in tears.

"That scoundrel, he must have got some more from outside and filled up the rack" said Deepen.

"Not possible" she said, "because each time the stock is entered, they keep records. But I'm sure that the stock I counted was less. I don't know how he did it".

Both Neil and Deepen looked at each other. They wanted to share their knowledge about the secret hide-out, the mysterious arrival and departure of cyanide-stocks. But this would expose their crimes.

Neil could not bear to see her tears and spoke in fear "we can share some information on this cyanide stock matter only if you promise to keep it a secret".

"What are you talking about?" she asked.

Then Neil and Deepen explained the entire episode to her about the stock of cyanide being hidden in the janitor's area.

On hearing the entire story, Anita's face was frozen. She did not speak for a minute and then got up from the table to quickly move out.

"This place is too risky to discuss. Meet me at the coffee shop this evening at 8," she said softly before leaving.

Deepen could not understand what was happening but evening coffee with Anita was an occasion Neil wasn't going to miss. He rushed home early pretending to have developed a stomachache. The plan was to get dressed for a meeting with Anita at the coffee shop. Too bad that even Deepen was going to come. He was hoping to be all alone with Anita.

That evening the trio met over coffee in the local cafe. Then she explained to them the plot, which, as per her understanding, was the truth.

"There is no doubt that Ramanuj is stealing the cyanide from the lab. But he does it in a planned way. He is first moving it out of the main storage area, which is under lock and key. Then he keeps it in a buffer zone, which is hidden from the main stock. Once the auditor gives the report on the correctness of the stock, he is then free to smuggle it out of the company. That could be the reason why my predecessor was asked to leave," she explained.

Neil was in a different world. He found Anita more attractive when she was talking about a serious matter.

"But Anita, you said that the item was not expensive, then what would he be getting by stealing it?" asked Deepen.

"Because, cyanide cannot be purchased directly, he is selling it at a very high price to criminals who use it to kill somebody or a terrorist who is planning a suicide mission. It is very dangerous to provide or supply cyanide to criminals." She was worried.

Neil suddenly realised that the only chance to impress Anita was by getting into a detective mode and help her solve this case. He had been reading a lot of detective novels.

"But there is a probability that Ramanuj is innocent. There could be another person who is hearing your conversation and acting accordingly." said Neil.

"Yes, probably, but then he would not react so strongly when I reported the shortage of cyanide. If he were innocent, he would cooperate with me and help me solve it. I remember that when he came to count the quantity, he was pretty confident that it was perfect," she replied.

"Why should we get in? All of us are qualified, we can get good jobs. To hell with Ramanuj and his gang of criminals!" said Deepen.

"Certainly not, we are responsible citizens, we must fight and solve this case," she yelled.

"Yeah, yeah, we should do it!" Neil was just staring at her pretty eyes. He had nothing to do with the case, but score over Deepen to win Anita.

The situation was dangerous. There was a strong possibility of criminal involvement. The risk was very high. Anita was thinking about all possible scenarios.

"Let us go and give the information to Patel," said Deepen.

"But not without proof!" said detective Neil, "we will go back to the janitor's room to see if he is using it again."

"I have a plan!" said Anita "you keep a close check on your secret area. If you see any stock movement, quickly inform me. I will reach there with him and check the stock in everybody's presence. If the stock is not correctly accounted, he will be questioned. The fresh stock has not reached, so our plan has to work."

"What if he says that the balance stock is in the janitor's room?" asked Deepen.

"Then he gets into bigger trouble because the cyanide stock cannot be stored without a double locked storage" said Anita.

"Wow, Anita, you are so intelligent!" said Neil. She responded with a sweet smile. Neil was in the seventh heaven.

The next day they both went back to the secret area to check if any stocks were kept. But the area was empty. The same day Anita also checked the system's stock. It was perfect, no discrepancy. Their enemy was cautious. At lunch they met again to re-think and if needed, rework the plan.

"Ramanuj is cautious. He will not take a chance now. So we will not be able to catch him red-handed," said Deepen.

"To catch our fish, we need bait" said Neil. He used to read a lot of detective novels during school. All that knowledge was coming back to him. For him it was necessary because Anita was quite appreciative of his suggestions.

"Anita, you must go on leave, because with you around, our enemy will make his move. Before going, you must tell us where the keys to the cyanide locker are kept. We will also need the system stock figures. So with you on leave, we will keep vigil" said Neil.

"So what will we do if our villain makes his move?" asked Deepen.

"We will first cause trouble for him and then launch our attack" said Neil "we will meet every evening to keep updating our plan." The plan had a provision for him to meet Anita every day.

In the next week, Anita took leave for a week. She informed Ramanuj that she probably would not be coming back. The boys kept a close check on the janitor's area.

Their plan was successful. On the third day, the polythene bags with cyanide were back in the same hiding spot. This time Neil and Deepen decided to take action. They first picked up the bags and changed the hiding spot. The janitor's area had many cupboards. They now hid it behind one of the cupboards. The space behind the wall and the cupboard could not be seen easily. It was foolproof. Ramanuj would now find it very difficult to locate the cyanide.

The trap was laid. Anita was happy that the boys were involved and were helping her do a good deed. She walked into the office the next day to check the stocks. The stock was lesser than the records. She now had proof. She called Ramanuj and showed him the discrepancy. His face grew red with anger. Meanwhile Neil and Deepen held a meeting with Patel. They told him the entire story. He was shocked.

They reached the heat treatment lab where Anita and Ramanuj were present. She showed Patel the shortage. Neil then went inside the janitor's area and brought the hidden stocks outside. He then kept the cyanide on the table. Anita added this to the main stock. It now tallied with the system stocks. The scam had been unearthed.

"I will conduct an enquiry into the entire matter" said Patel, "till then Ramanuj, you are suspended." Ramanuj did not say a word. He just put his head down and walked out of the lab. He picked up his bag and left. Patel then called the three of them into his office.

"I am glad that you guys did a fantastic job. Thank you so much. You saved the company from big trouble" he said. "But, I have a request. We will have to keep this information amongst ourselves. If the authorities come to know about this loophole, our cyanide procurement will come under the scanner. This will lead to production delays. Our company will lose its prime customer."

"We do understand sir. Our objective was to ensure that the wrong-doing comes to an end. We are happy that you have taken immediate action by suspending Ramanuj." said Anita.

The trio was successful. They had done it. Mission accomplished. The celebrations began at the local disco. The three were having a good time. It was then time for Neil to ask Deepen to leave early so that he could pop the question.

She said yes. They were in love with each other. The office was now a great place to work for Neil. Deepen was happy for his friends. Every day they had lunch and coffee together. Neil was on top of the world. He had a good job, a pretty girl and a bright future. He was planning to inform his family. They were very broadminded. He was sure they would accept Anita. Her family was a little conservative. She felt that it would be better if Neil's family first came forward with a formal proposal.

Sometimes what we plan does not happen. What actually happens is that which was never thought of at all. When life turns 180 degrees, all your plans fail. It makes you completely clueless on what to do. These are testing times for leaders. At such times you have to hold your ground, stay firm and fight back.

The last day of the Induction was followed by another surprise test conducted by Patel. The test was tough, but not irrelevant. It contained questions on all the departments that had been covered during the Induction. For those who were serious about the training, the exam was not difficult. But for Neil and Deepen it was a disaster. Neil failed the test. Playing games, falling in love and unearthing a scam were activities during Induction. But Deepen had displayed greater intelligence. He had given correct answers to many questions. He too however, had been declared a failure. Neil was upset. Deepen was angry. He had never failed in his life. After the results were declared Patel summoned both of them into his office.

"Sorry boys, we will not be able to confirm your appointment. Your failure has forced us to take this action. Your probation period will be extended with a warning letter. This would be your first and last extension. You would now need to be very careful because another mistake and the company will be issuing a Letter of Termination," said Patel.

It was a difficult situation. Deepen, unable to take this failure and humiliation, was frightfully frustrated.

"I'm not continuing in this stupid company," he told Neil "I will resign and move back to Kolkata. I am sure I'll get a job elsewhere or join my father."

"Don't be silly" said Neil, "We deserve it. A penal action by the company is not the end of life. We'll accept punishment and double our efforts to impress Patel."

"Just shut up, I'm not here to impress anybody. I've always been a performer. My paper was not checked properly. I will demand an explanation" Deepen was in a mood to fight.

Neil tried his best to convince him, but Deepen being egotistic, continued to be stubborn. It was his first academic failure in life. He had always scored well in school and college. He was proud of his knowledge. The humiliation of failure in his colleagues' presence wasn't something he was prepared to handle. He had made up his mind to fight. He asked Neil for support.

"No my friend, I can support you in all the small crimes that we did, but not for going against the system. My values tell me that you have to accept punishment when you make a mistake.

Patel has the right to punish us. Fighting back would be wrong. Playing mischief is okay with me but I cannot support you with what, according to me, is unethical," said Neil.

For the first time both friends had a difference of opinion. They shook hands and decided to part ways. The next day Deepen walked into Patel's office. He demanded that Patel show him his answer sheet. Patel was angry. He refused to part with the answer sheet. Deepen was prepared for this and placed his resignation on the table. Patel accepted it immediately. He called the HR officer and asked him to bring Deepen's relieving letter carrying today's date. That afternoon, Deepen walked out of the company's gates for the last time. Neil was down with grief. It had all happened so fast. He had lost a friend, got almost fired and was not in a position to approach Anita's family without a permanent job in hand. Life had taken a U-turn. He shut his eyes. Many thoughts came to his mind together.

His dream was shattered. The other trainees looked down upon him. Some of them also told him on his face that he deserved it. Office humiliation is a difficult situation. Very few employees can handle it. Neil was strong by heart. He could not only handle it, but was ready to accept the toughest challenge to win against the odds and win his girl with pride. He gathered courage and went up to meet Patel. Patel was in his chair with a strange smile on his face. It was the first time Neil was seeing Patel in this avataar.

"So you also plan to resign just like your friend?" asked Patel.

"No sir. I accept your penal action. I apologize for my conduct. Yes, I know I have not been taking things seriously. I have failed. I deserve it. But I will change. I promise you. In the next three months, you will change your opinion about me. I assure you," said Neil.

"My dear boy," said Patel "I never change my opinion. In the next six months, you will be out of PP Alloys. I am not interested in your apology. Please use this time to look out for another job"

Patel's words were like hot needles, but Neil was already deeply wounded. He put his head down and walked out of Patel's office.

PP Alloys was owned by Prakash Pillai who was also the Managing Director. There were two people in the organisation who were very close to him. The first was Patel who was his right hand and the second was Sanjiv Rai the Marketing Head. It was Patel and Sanjiv who managed the entire company. Sanjiv was a dynamic leader, a man of action. The sales, branding team, business development and Research and Design department reported to him. The business began at Sanjiv's desk. A product or a customer was listed. Research was done, and a problem area identified. A technical or commercial solution was designed and tried. Once successful, it then came to Patel for production at the lowest possible cost.

Traditionally in most of the companies, Marketing and Production are rivals. In PP Alloys, Patel and Sanjiv were not just rivals, they were sworn enemies. They hated each other. Both thought the other wasn't efficient enough. Neil discovered this fact when he met Sanjiv for the first time.

"Don't worry my friend. Failure in Induction doesn't mean much. You have been hired for Business Development. Here, a relationship, an idea, plays an important role. It is okay if you don't know the processes very well. Just focus on the market, keep close contact with customers. I am sure that you will do well" advised Sanjiv.

Neil could understand that because he had been Sanjiv's choice during recruitment that Patel was his formal enemy. Therefore, there was a probability that he would still do well if he chose to impress Sanjiv. He therefore pushed himself focusing on marketing. It was no longer just a job but a fight for survival. He had informed Anita that unless he was made permanent, he would make no further move in their relationship. Deepen was no longer present in this challenge because he was already in Kolkata.

In his new work profile, Neil had to travel extensively. He was continuously visiting customers, trying to understand their requirements, entertaining them at dinner parties etc. During one such visit, he was in Mumbai with a customer in a five star hotel for dinner. They were discussing a new application over a drink. The place was very crowded and noisy. He was down with two beers and felt the need to use the washroom. Walking towards the door, he suddenly saw a familiar person enter. It was Ramanuj. He was well dressed. The steward was escorting him towards a small table reserved for him. Neil was shocked to see a suspended officer of PP Alloys enjoying dinner at a five star hotel in Mumbai. He was now confident that Ramanuj was involved in much bigger crimes.

As Ramanuj sat at his table, the waiter approached him immediately, paying special attention to his every command. It appeared that he was a regular and probably a heavy tipper. He then took out his mobile phone and charger. The waiter took it from his hand for charging. Neil was hiding behind a pillar. He knew that Ramanuj was probably meeting some criminals or just blowing away money ill-earned. A great idea struck Neil. If he could manage to get hold of his mobile phone, the last dialled list would have some numbers. These would surely be some criminals. It would give him a lead to crack a big case.

The waiter had taken his mobile phone to a switch panel near the main counter, away from the table where Ramanuj was seated. The counter was manned by the hotel manager along with two or three staff members. It was also the main cash counter. It was impossible to take the phone in front of them. Neil was desperate. Solving this case would give him a reason to be proud of himself. Since Ramanuj had already been suspended, there was no fear. But if he was caught, Ramanuj would probably beat him up. When the rewards are big, the risk is bigger. Neil decided to go for it.

He confidently walked towards the main counter and said "Ramanuj sir wants his mobile for a minute. Please give it to me." His voice was strong and commanding.

Nobody messes with a regular customer and the manager immediately handed the mobile to Neil. He took it to the corner to see the last dialled numbers. The light was dim, Neil was excited. What happened next gave him a 440 volt shock. It was impossible to believe that the last dialled number was of a person so familiar to him.

It was Patel. Neil was numb. Ramanuj was talking to Patel just before entering the hotel. There were also other numbers. His last received list also had a couple of Patel's calls. Neil quickly returned the mobile to the counter. He returned to his own table. His customer had ordered some more drinks. Neil had lost his interest in the dinner or drinks. His mind was confused. Patel was regularly communicating with a suspended employee. Was he also involved? Was he trying to patch up with Ramanuj? These were the questions in his mind. However it was Patel who had suspended Ramanuj. If they were connected, why would he associate himself with Ramanuj? It was strange. He also had a thought that probably Patel was just acting as a tough guy and was the main villain. That is the reason why he had probably failed Deepen in the test along with me, thought Neil.

Next day, he came back to Pune and met Anita. He told her the entire episode. She was also surprised. It was difficult for both of them to imagine that Patel was the main villain. It was sad but true.

"What if Patel is hatching a plot to catch Ramanuj red handed? What if Ramanuj is giving threatening calls to Patel for giving him a clean chit? Why would Patel commit a crime ? He is a good man," insisted Anita.

"I have no idea. But unknowingly we have touched something very big. The risk is also very high. We could be taking on big criminals. I am on a weak wicket because Patel has already put me on extended probation. Which means that one mistake and I will be fired," said Neil.

Anita's next assignment was in the HR department where she was conducting an audit on hiring expenditures. She was continuously thinking about Patel. Anxiety was killing her. She decided to take a risk. She entered the area of personnel files and took out Ramanuj's file. He was in service for the last five years. He had been recommended by Patel, hired by Patel, promoted three times by Patel. By qualification he was just a graduate. Hired as an office clerk, in five years, Patel had promoted him to the post of Head of Department. But the most shocking fact was that there was no suspension letter in his file. The personal file of every employee is like a single point of information about his service record.

She met Neil in the coffee shop that evening. Patel's nexus with Ramanuj was confirmed. He was a secret partner in the crime or probably was the mastermind who was sucking the blood out of PP Alloys. It was also revealed why he just threw him out of the company without officially suspending him through a letter.

"What should I do?" asked Neil.

"Fight back, expose them, tell Sanjiv" said Anita.

"I can't do it. Patel is too strong in this organization. We also do not know how many other employees are involved. We do not know the size of the scam and worst of all I am weak, very weak. Patel is waiting to find a reason to terminate my appointment. Unless I put forth a significant performance, he may not make me permanent," said Neil.

"But you can always get another job, why stay with bad guys?" Anita responded.

"It is not about good or bad, it is not about changing jobs, it is about winning. I may leave this organisation but as a winner and not a loser" said Neil. "Sometimes in life, we have to choose our battles. If we decide to fight all battles that come our way, we may lose all of them. Even if we win a few, our energy will be drained in fighting so many battles."

"I respect your decision and hope that we succeed in convincing our parents for us to get married," said Anita.

He just smiled and left. Maturity was kicking in. Neil had broken out of the secure shell of college life. He had now entered the real world. His thought process had changed along with his habits. He had now stopped fooling around at work. He was well-focused on his job. He was now concentrated on getting more product knowledge, meeting more customers, reading books and keeping himself abreast with the latest technology. In the office he did not let go of any opportunity to impress Patel as well as Sanjiv. He wanted to get into their good books.

In the next 3 months, Neil managed to secure his first big order. It was easy for Sanjiv to confirm his appointment. Patel could not object this time. By the end of the year, Neil had managed to win "The Best Sales Employee of The Year" award. His dedication and hard work were far above the rest. Both families approved their relationship and he was now officially engaged to Anita. Life was smooth and comfortable.

Patel was in continuous touch with Ramanuj. Their nexus was in good health. Ramanuj had floated a new trading company. Neil was keeping a watch on his movement. He had sent in his resignation and it was accepted by Patel. Ramanuj had now started supplying raw materials to PP Alloys. Neil was confident that Patel was making money out of this supply. But he just kept on making observations.

As Neil posted his award on his CV, job offers started pouring in and he began to attend interviews. When you work with dedication, knowledge comes automatically. This eventually gets noticed in interviews and creates a long lasting impression on potential hirers. Neil was happy to receive an appointment offer from a very large multinational at a salary hike of 40% over his current package. This increment would now help him buy his first home. He was excited and decided to quit PP Alloys. But his desire to attack Patel was pending. He sent a confirmation to the new company with a message that he would be joining after a month.

Neil was no longer weak in Patel's presence. He had proven himself and the best part was that he had nothing to lose because of the new job that he had secured. All he needed was solid proof to corner Patel. Neil had some college mates working in the mobile company who could give him an itemized bill of Patel's mobile phone. The bill taken was from the month when he had unofficially suspended Ramanuj. From Patel's bill it was obvious that he was making multiple calls every day to Ramanuj. Why would a department head talk so much with a suspended employee? His second proof was the fact that no suspension letter had been served on Ramanuj and the third fact was that a suspended employee had been inducted as a key vendor.

With hiding no longer required, he directly approached Sanjiv and told him the full story. It was a Saturday evening and he expected Sanjiv to think, plan and set his attack on Monday.

Sanjiv looked happy instead of getting worried. He now had a chance to attack his arch rival in the company. He took the bill copy and approached Patel directly. Neil wanted to hear the drama and followed him. He entered Patel's cabin. Neil quickly put his ear on the door. It was a Saturday evening and most employees had left for the day.

"So you have come prepared with proof this time?" he heard Patel, "what do we do about all the extra third party commission that you have been gobbling up my dear Sanjiv, and do you want me to also expose your relationship with your past secretary who almost committed suicide because of your abuse ?"

Neil was shocked. Sanjiv was also deeply involved. Both were in the same boat.

"The boy knows too much. You will be in trouble if the boy goes to Mr. Pillai" said Sanjiv "and once you are in trouble, I will also not be able to play my games. So what do we do now?" The question carried no solutions.

"Don't worry, I have my contacts. The boy will be behind bars before Monday" said Patel, "Just pretend to take action against me. We will plant drugs in his house and then send the cops to nab him."

Neil ran out towards Sanjiv's cabin. He quickly typed out his resignation and emailed it to Sanjeev requesting early action. He then waited for Sanjiv to return.

"I have nailed him, you were right, he is a fraud. I guess he will resign on Monday," said Sanjiv.

Neil tried his best to hide his emotions and remain stable. "What is the point sir; I do not see any victory by defeating Patel. This is not my battle. It is your wish on what is to be done but I have decided to resign from this company. I will not continue," said Neil.

"Oh, it is such a loss to lose a good employee like you, but if you have made up your mind I will not stop you. Please hand over all your pending work to my assistant." said Sanjiv.

That was his last evening in PP Alloys. Neil moved out and joined the new company; he married Anita and was blessed with a pretty girl within the next two years. He named her Deepa.

Some of you may call him a coward. You also may think that he should have at least written to the Managing Director after resigning. We all take decisions in life. Some of them turn out to be right and others become the wrong ones. Neil definitely could have helped in solving the case by putting his life at stake. He could have approached the police for protection. There was a probability that he could have won against them and become a local hero. But Neil did not do any such thing. The reason was best known to him. He decided to leave that mess and start a new life.

On Deepa's tenth birthday, Neil was travelling for work out of India. He opened his laptop to send her birthday greetings. His inbox had two new emails; one informing him of his promotion to the post of Assistant Vice President and the second was a news flash about PP Alloys having gone bankrupt.

"Happy Birthday to my lovely daughter Deepa," he began writing the email with a broad smile on his face.

Notes

You Were Born To Do It

It was a beautiful deep blue sea with multi-coloured shining fish swimming within the corals. He approached a large school of clown fish. They scattered away as he came near them. The water's temperature was perfect. Diving in, in the Great Barrier Reef, Australia is like floating in paradise. He wanted to see more but the oxygen supply on the diving suit indicated a warning for him to turn back. As he turned, a sharp pointed rock ripped open his leg with a wide cut.

"Ammaaa" he yelled out under the water, creating a lot of bubbles. The bubbles were in Tamil, because they emanated from the mouth of Mr. Ramachandra Venkatpalli Padhmanaban, a permanent resident of Chennai. Blood attracted sharks and he had to rush back immediately to the boat. The distance to the boat was approximately 10 minutes. He was tense and began praying fervently to lord Tirupathi "I want to see Amma again," he thought as he kept swimming fast with a terribly sharp pain in his leg.

Prayers to Amma helped and he made it just in time to reach the boat before the sharks could get him. It was a relief as he sat in the boat. Medication was provided by the organizers and he considered himself lucky to be alive. "You keep making new mistakes every time mate, this sport looks difficult for you," said the instructor.

"But I love deep-sea diving!" he said.

"Well, it looks like diving is not your cup of tea. You should try something else," the instructor retorted.

We always like to try out new things that seem nice. There is nothing wrong in doing different things but only as a hobby, not as a full-time profession. We all keep boarding different trains in life and wait for the station of our choice. But the station of our choice never comes when we are in the wrong train. It is therefore very important that we understand our strengths, decide our destination, board the correct train and wait till the desired station arrives without alighting at any other station.

Ramachandra Venkatpalli Padhmanaban was a happy soul. This tall dark and handsome boy was known as Paddy to all. He was studying management in Brisbane, Australia. Born and brought up in Chennai, Paddy had found Brisbane a great place to live. He was truly enjoying his life which included Management Education and fun during weekends. At his college, Paddy was a bright student. He could easily manage studies along with diving, snorkelling etc. on weekends.

Paddy hailed from a traditional business family from Chennai. His father owned a shop in Pondy bazaar. The shop had a great reputation. It was a magnet for women. It had a humungous variety of saris, dresses, imitation jewellery etc. Paddy's grandfather had started this shop. It was a prominent landmark in Pondy bazaar. Women used to spend hours in this shop. They were entertained with respect. Salesmen here were trained to continuously keep showing materials to the ladies without getting tired.

As a school boy, Paddy used to spend a lot of time after school in the shop. He would finish his homework in an hour and then have lots of spare time. He used to observe girls and ladies making purchases. It was very amusing for him. His favourite game was to predict purchases by buyers. He initially waited at the entrance. As a customer walked in, he would predict that she would be purchasing a sari. He would then follow the customer to that section. His predictions' accuracy used to be 50%. Once a lady or a young girl sat across a salesman to see various items he would predict, often accurately what she was going to buy. He would closely observe the special twinkle in her eye when she saw a product that appealed to her.

Customers generally do not like somebody continuously observing them but Paddy was just a small boy. They found it amusing and did not object when Paddy stared openly at them. The sales persons working in the shop were from the neighbouring suburbs of Chennai. They were men and women who were not highly educated. They worked on a fixed salary. Their working style was mechanical. As a customer approached, they kept displaying products till the customer confirmed her purchase. Then they had to once again fold and keep the items back on the shelves.

Many times, Paddy would understand that the salesman was not showing the woman customer what she was looking for and eventually the customer would get up and leave the shop. He would then go to the salesman to explain to him why the customer had left without making any purchase. The salesman would simply smile and ignore his advice. He would even share his observations with his father, who would change the subject by asking him about his studies. Nobody took Paddy seriously. His observations remained with him. However, Paddy was not to be bothered. For him it was a good game which he kept on playing. A few years of practice and Paddy had become a champion. His predictions used to be almost 100% right. He could also differentiate between a serious customer and somebody who came to the shop only to browse. Paddy's game continued till he was thirteen. His father could understand the rising demands of studies in school and stopped him from coming to the shop. He appointed tuition teachers who came home to teach Paddy. His father knew the importance of education and wanted Paddy to get the best of it. Paddy was an above-average student. With special tuitions, his academic scores improved. Paddy scored well in school as well as college to secure admission in Chemical Engineering. Submissions, journals and practical work took a toll on his time. Paddy was extremely busy with his course curriculum. The shop was forgotten. It was just a fun memory.

Paddy's attachment to his mother was very strong. His mother used to feed him with her own hands till he was 12. He used to sleep beside her till he was 14. She was a loving mother who would shower affection on Paddy, her only child. Paddy's birth had taken place after two tragic miscarriages. He was therefore very special to her. She would spend a lot of time readying his clothes, arranging his books, setting up his school bag etc. Her love for Paddy had made him a mamma's boy. At 18, Paddy was still dependant on his mother for basic things. This was a big worry for his father who wanted Paddy to become independent.

After finishing Chemical Engineering, he urged Paddy to take admission in a management institute outside India. Paddy was excited to see the college campus on the internet but staying away from his mother was a big problem. She was against Paddy going away from home. Paddy's father was however successful in cutting the cord that tied Paddy to his mother. He convinced his wife that Paddy had to become independent and higher education in a foreign country was very important. He promised Paddy a motorbike only if he went abroad. The mother and son became weak once again as the day of departure arrived. But Paddy's father was a good salesman. He used his skills to ensure that the decision did not change. Paddy's flight finally took off.

Brisbane is a beautiful city. It has a good mix of the city, the country side and is near the pristine beaches of the Great Barrier Reef. Within a few weeks, Paddy began to like his new lifestyle. The weather was not like Chennai. The girls were prettier. Paddy also got an opportunity to join a group of chemical engineers. He made friends with members of both the sexes. Besides studying during weekdays, he also started taking lessons in deep-sea diving on weekends with some of his physically fit friends. He let himself loose to enjoy life. Australia helped him acclimatize to non-vegetarian food, alcohol and smoking. The first year ended with Paddy securing very good marks. He left for Chennai for a short visit before starting the final year.

His mother was in tears at the airport. She was overjoyed to meet her son. But Paddy was no longer the same. He had changed. Paddy was no longer her baby. Chennai suddenly appeared very hot, humid and filthy for Paddy. The girls looked over dressed. The food was too spicy. Spending two weeks became difficult. He was glad when they came to an end. Paddy's father was proud to see his score and became prouder on knowing that his son was becoming independent.

"I am sure that you will do better than me in the shop" said Paddy's father, just before starting on a delicious family dinner.

"Shop, oh our shop!" fumbled Paddy with morsels of rice falling from his mouth. He suddenly remembered that they had a shop that was responsible for the great life to which he was entitled. The shop was the family's only source of revenue.

"Of course yes, our shop is waiting to get a talented owner like you. I am glad to have sent you abroad. Hope you will get some exposure on running shops in Australia," he helped himself to a large serving of rice.

"Dad, I do not have any plans to return. I will take up a job or start a chemical based business in Australia!" said Paddy shocking his parents.

The scenario at the dinner table changed. The conversation became hotter than the 'rasam' being served with the rice. The arguments continued throughout the night, depriving his parents of their much needed sleep. But Paddy had made up his mind. He was now independent. His mother set up her emotional attack. Father was angry. Paddy was scared. His funding for the second year was due. The risk was big. His father could stop the show immediately ensuring that he would never return. He finally surrendered before them and promised to return on completing his studies. His father was smart. He wanted to be doubly sure and therefore suspended Paddy's credit card. Paddy was given an account with just enough money to pay his fees and barely manage his expenditure for a year.

When Paddy was back in Brisbane, he understood that his weekend parties would have to end. The money was not enough for him to have a good time. But he was a free man in Brisbane. He decided to take up a part-time job in a super market. Paddy would now attend classes in the day and work in the super-market in the evenings. The pay was not good enough but it certainly covered those expenses that gave him a good weekend. The only setback was that his grades were not very high. The second year's subjects were tough. His professors were concerned. They tried to coax Paddy to work harder but without success.

The supermarket was a big place owned by Mark Baker. In the first week of work, Paddy was very low. He was sad that he had to work in the evening instead of studying or just hanging around with his friends. He dragged himself to work. Mark did not like a dull boy at work. He looked at him and called him to his office. But on hearing Paddy's story, he let out a loud laugh.

"A rich Indian boy working to have fun, interesting!" he said, "It's okay, mate."

He was still very sad. Mark got up from his seat and putting his hand on Paddy's shoulder continued, "Look mate, if you

111

think sad, you will be sad, if you be sad, it will cause pain. But if you can think happy when you are in pain, even the pain will reduce. So just be happy and enjoy every part of your life"

Mark had actually made a mark on Paddy's mind. It is so true that our thinking steers our day. It makes us happy or sad. It is the way we look at life. Think positive, feel positive and keep smiling. That was Mark's motto in life. It made his store a great place to shop for his customers. It was the experience of shopping here that made them come back again and again.

Paddy broke through his shell of grief and immersed himself in the job. Paddy had always been a customer's face reader. He requested Mark to assign him the role of customer support. In this job Paddy had to wait for a customer to ask for support. He wore a big patch of "Ask Me For Help!". He kept moving near the shelves looking for customers who appeared confused or were staring at the goods. On spotting a target, he would approach the customer to offer help and ensure that the customer got the right product. Paddy also kept a close check on the products that were nearing expiry dates. He would inform Mark accordingly so that a discount could be offered on them.

Paddy was in action, he had picked up his special talent again. He could actually face read the Aussies. They liked him and started asking for Paddy on their next visit. Mark was thrilled. He became Paddy's fan. The day started with Mark asking Paddy what items to keep on the entry shelves. His sales increased and inventory was very well managed. Mark's revenue increased. He therefore increased Paddy's pay cheque. Paddy was on daily wages. When Mark gave him a raise on his per-day income, Paddy actually requested for a Friday off. The amount was now good enough for him to work only four days a week. He had three days for having fun. Mark was not comfortable with Paddy working only four days but couldn't help it. Paddy was important to him even if he came only four days a week.

Paddy's next agenda was to find a fulltime job of his choice, one that matched his qualifications. He was sure to betray his parents. Going back to Chennai and managing his father's shop was not his choice. His interest was in the chemical business and staying in the land of fun. Paddy had made many friends in college. Most of them were from Australia and surrounding Asian countries. He often helped many of them complete their assignments. They liked Paddy but never made him their best friend. Paddy also did not endeavour to make best friends. He often mentioned his interest to Mark who had a friend Roger Kane, in the business of recycling material. He referred Paddy to Roger. Mark actually wanted Paddy to partner with himself but decided to help Paddy pursue his own interest.

Roger was the owner of a big recycling business. Roger's firm collected a lot of waste and recycled it. Before recycling, it was important to separate different types of materials. There were chemical and mechanical processes involved. Mark took Paddy to Roger's factory. They both saw the premises. Paddy was thrilled to see his setup. As a chemical engineer from a premier institute of India, Paddy could also make useful suggestions to Roger. He spent a day at the plant. By the time Paddy left, Roger was highly impressed. He decided to offer Paddy a full time job. The salary was decent. Paddy could easily stay in a back packer's lodge and make enough money to make a decent living in Brisbane. Roger also mentioned that he would pay a bonus to Paddy if he could make any revenue increment in his business.

Paddy was not able to secure a good score in the final exam, barely managing to pass. The greatest difficulty was now how to break the bad news to his parents about him not returning to Chennai. For a difficult assignment, you need a creative idea. Efforts have to be taken and risk needs to be minimized. Paddy suddenly got a brainwave. With the left-over spare cash that he had, Paddy purchased two tickets for his parents to visit Brisbane. He called home and requested them to visit his two year home once before returning to India. They gladly agreed. Paddy booked a hotel for them. He had briefed Mark and Roger to brainwash them into allowing Paddy to continue living in Brisbane. The plan was foolproof.

The plane coming from Chennai landed in Brisbane after a two-hour halt at Singapore. It was the first journey abroad for Mr. and Mrs. Padhmanaban. They were frustrated with the overnight flight journey. They were exhausted as they walked out of the aircraft. The first shock that came their way was that Mr. Padhmanaban was fined 50 Australian dollars for speaking on the mobile phone while passing through Immigration. The second shock came when food being carried by Mrs. Padhmanaban was thrown into the dustbin by the Airport Lady Security Officer.

"Scoundrels, rascals, crooks!" said Mrs. Padhmanaban. She was brutally hurt to see her delicacies with pure ghee landing in the dustbin.

When they met Paddy the smile came back. But it was temporary.

"We take the bus," said Paddy, as he took their bags.

"No, we will take a taxi" said his dad.

"This is Australia, Appa, taxis are very expensive," replied Paddy.

"Scoundrels, rascals, crooks!" said Mr. Padhmanaban "they are cheaters, these Aussies....."

"As if your Chennai autos are saints!" laughed Paddy.

This was a big mistake. The Tamil words which followed later were at a very high decibel, enough to attract the attention of the crowd. He somehow managed to drop them at the hotel and reached his hostel. It was a bad start and his plans were crumbling. He thought that they would get impressed with Brisbane as he had been. They would fall in love with the cleanliness, the friendly people, the food etc. In fact his mother refused to touch food for two days thinking about the rascal airport security girl. They also refused to meet or discuss with any more of Paddy's white friends. Both sulked in the hotel room, awaiting their date of departure back home to Chennai.

"Amma and Appa, I will not be returning to Chennai. I have a job in Brisbane and will live here forever!" he was just practicing his dialogues with Roger and Mark.

"I can't do this," he said, "They will react with emotion. I had promised them last year to return and now I'm betraying them. Actually I betrayed them last year."

Mark was intelligent. He knew that Paddy would not be able to handle the situation. Plus the reception of the couple in Australia was not warm. They had already developed a sickness in his disease-free country. But Paddy was a friend and he needed help.

Mark invited the Padhmanabans to dinner at his place. Paddy had given him a full briefing about the culture and definition of strictly vegetarian food. But Paddy's parents refused. They were vegetarians. They were aware that Mark ate beef. So the proposal had been rejected. However Mark was determined to help Paddy.

The venue was changed to an Indian restaurant. They agreed and accepted his invitation. During the meal, Mark had set up with the waiter to add some vodka to Paddy's fruit drink. After 3 drinks, Paddy broke the ice and the vodka started talking. A heated discussion began. Mark and Roger were focusing on expressions and body-language. The entire discussion was in Tamil. Mark could understand that the mother was upset, the father was angry and the son was determined. The vodka had done its job. Mission accomplished!

Paddy's parents packed their bags. Mark reached them to the airport. Paddy was standing at the gate. They did not look at him and entered the airport without a good-bye.

Roger had some friends who worked at the airport. He had made arrangements to ensure Paddy's parents didn't get into any trouble on their way back to India. Paddy was upset that his parents had to leave, but was also excited on entering his newly-chosen world.

Paddy moved to a bachelor hostel and started working with Roger. The Padhmanaban couple was back in Chennai. At work, Paddy took a lot of interest in learning concepts. He was looking at optimising processes. He found that Roger had added unnecessary automatic processes. This had increased maintenance schedules. He prepared a time motion analysis of the processes.

That unfortunate weekend, Paddy was working. He was fine-tuning his report. He was also unwell and nervous but blamed his work-related stress for his condition. Something felt wrong - he started getting an uncomfortable feeling. It was strange. There was no reason to be so disturbed. But he was certainly not normal.

He could not sleep the entire night on Saturday. At 4.00 in the morning, he received a call from India. His father was no more having suffered a massive heart attack and was declared dead at the hospital. Paddy was shocked. He sat on his chair. First he did not cry and then suddenly tears began to flow. He packed his bags, wrote a note to Roger and rushed to the airport to take the next flight to Chennai.

From the airport he took a taxi straight home. His house was full of people. His relatives had made arrangements to keep the body till his arrival. The funeral was undertaken by the priest as per rituals. It was a very long process. Paddy somehow managed to complete all the steps with continuous guidance from the priest. He felt exhausted and slept the whole day.

Paddy's father was history. It was difficult for Paddy to adjust to these new circumstances. The pain in his heart of not saying a final goodbye to Appa was now a permanent wound.

For the next two weeks, Paddy was only seeing visitors who wanted to pay their respects to the family. His mother was completely down. The doctor had put her on pills. Odd looking priests were visiting their home every day reciting prayers. Unseen relatives were staying with them. The house had turned into a bazaar.

"Suresh anna is here to see you" said his servant. Suresh was their shop's supervisor. Suresh had been taking care of the shop these past two weeks.

"Good morning sir!" said Suresh. He stood up when Paddy walked into the living room. It was an indication that Paddy was the new boss. He had never stood up on Paddy's entering before. Paddy asked Suresh to take a seat. Paddy's mother also walked in for a discussion. They both wanted Paddy to take charge of the shop.

"Your father worked hard all his life. Our shop is now a land-mark in Pondy bazaar. The time has come for you to take it ahead" said his mother. Paddy was irritated. Nobody was ever interested in what he wanted to do in life. First it was his father and now his mother. Life was just a big obligation.

He suddenly thought of a unique idea. The shop was any way functioning for two weeks without his father. Why not delegate the job to a good manager like Suresh? Discussing with his mother would lead to obvious results. Therefore he decided to take the reins in his own hands.

"Suresh, I want you to run the shop for us. I will only come on weekends to check the accounts" said Paddy "can you do it for us?"

Suresh had a big smile on his face. It was what he had always wanted. Paddy's mother left the room. She stopped talking to her son. She was already in grief and this decision of Paddy's pained her even more. She never asked Paddy what he was going to do with his life. She also expected him to go back to Brisbane leaving her all alone in Chennai. Too much tension and lack of proper eating habits had made her collapse into unconsciousness. The doctor advised complete rest and medical attention due to very low blood pressure.

Paddy was upset. He was also very emotional. He kept thinking about his father who had most probably died thinking of his son. His mother was now sick because her son was not going to walk in his father's footsteps.

"Why can't they just let me do what I want to do?" yelled Paddy on the phone with Roger who was the only one who had understood Paddy's dilemma. He loved his mother and his job equally. Paddy was being torn into pieces. He also received a call from Mark. Speaking to Mark was a big relief.

"Why don't you start Roger's business in Chennai?" asked Mark.

"What a brilliant idea!" exclaimed Paddy. He knew that recycling was a manually intensive industry and Australian labourers charged ten times the salary of those in Chennai. All he had to do was import waste into India, process it and send it back or sell it in India. He immediately spoke to Roger. He liked the idea. Paddy had a smile on his face after many days. He went to his mother and informed her about the change of plans.

"Amma, I'm not going back to Brisbane. I will settle down in Chennai" he said while sitting next to her sick bed.

His mother felt better. Her son wasn't going back after all and would live with her in Chennai. The effect was strong enough to restore her lost health.

Chennai has a booming auto industry with ancillary units. Lots of manufacturing was happening around the place. Auto components were manufactured by many mid-sized companies. Paddy conducted a survey. He found out about the buyers of scrap and their business models. Recycling was not done in most of the cases. Paddy was excited. He now needed land and investment. Management students are good at making business plans. Paddy's business plan was appreciated by scrap dealers and some other corporate buyers. Roger was also impressed with proposed profitability figures. He decided to be the investor and booked his tickets to visit Chennai.

Roger's first visit to India gave him a culture shock. The spicy Indian food destroyed his digestion. Lack of beef was a problem. The vast crowds were too scary for him. But he maintained his decision of opening a unit with Paddy as partner. The plan was simple. Roger would send containers of Australian scrap to India. Then Paddy's team would manually separate the two or three materials. This cleaned scrap would be sold in the manufacturing market. Paddy wanted a mega launch party for his business, but Roger refused. He was a seasoned businessman. Before starting a company or making an agreement, he insisted on a pilot project. He went back to Brisbane and organised the dispatch of three cartons of scrap to Chennai.

Paddy's homework was good but not complete. He had not checked on the Indian customs department before making this business plan. Import of such scrap into India was not allowed. The local customs agent assured Paddy that there would not be any problem getting his goods out of the Indian customs. He was confident of getting the goods released.

With a green signal from Paddy, the consignment was shipped from Brisbane, taking three weeks to reach Chennai. As per the agent's instructions the documents carried names of spare parts. They had not declared the consignment as scrap. Customs duty was therefore paid accordingly. It appeared that Paddy's life was finally moving in the right direction.

"Hello! Am I speaking to Mr. Ramachandra Venkatpalli Padhmanaban?" it was a lady's voice on the phone at 11.00 on a Monday morning. "I am Padmalaxmi Iyer, Chennai Customs Appraising Officer."

"Yes, madam, what can I do for you?" asked Paddy. She ordered him to reach her office immediately. Her voice was firm. Paddy rushed to her office in the Chennai Customs office without informing or calling the agent.

The customs office was a busy place with people running around with bunches of papers. They all appeared very busy. Lots of files stuffed with papers were lying around. He searched for her name and saw it written outside a small cabin. There was a queue waiting to meet Padmalaxmi. Paddy had to wait for an hour before he could enter her office.

"Must be a stuffy grumpy old lady!" Paddy thought. She had sounded very bossy on the phone. He was actually a little afraid of approaching her directly. But she did not give him any choice.

As the bell rang, Paddy entered her cabin. She was seated in a big chair. His eyes popped out. His heart skipped a beat. Paddy's brain had frozen.

She was amazing. She was the most beautiful girl he had ever seen in his life. His mind went blank as he kept staring at her and couldn't speak a word. She was in a sari. Her hair was tightly bound with white flowers. The flowers were fresh and the fragrance ever so romantic.

"Yes, what is your case number?" she asked. He stared at her without replying. She banged the files in her hand. She repeated her question. He fumbled with his name.

"I have checked your consignment. It is scrap and not spares. This is a case of mis-declaration. You can go behind bars. Do you want to go to jail?" she asked.

"I want to have coffee with you!" words were just coming out from his mouth. He was out of control.

"Look mister, bribing is a serious offense. Don't you believe in the law?" she replied.

"Don't you believe in love at first sight?" asked Paddy. He hadn't realized that what he was saying or wanting to do was highly improper.

"What nonsense, how can you say such things in my office?" She got wild.

"I agree" said Paddy, still in a numb state "I will ask pop my question on our first date."

She was furious and yelled loudly. The guard sitting outside came in and asked Paddy to get out.

"Bye dear, looking forward to meet you again!" said Paddy with a big smile on his face as the security guard pulled him out of her cabin.

The officer was upset. She issued a "show cause notice" to him. As he came out of the office, Paddy realised his blunder. He called his agent and narrated the incident.

"You are a mad man Mr. Paddy!" the agent reacted.

Paddy's customs agent was upset with him for going to her directly. He somehow managed the situation by paying off the fine and penalty. The next day, both of them went to see Padmalaxmi. He made Paddy apologize. She was still upset. The agent tried his best to calm her. They pleaded guilty and asked for mercy. She calmed down a bit and assured them that there would not be an arrest and placed an order to cancel his import number.

Paddy had lost a huge amount of money in the matter. He also received a call from Roger cancelling his plans to invest in India. Paddy's customs agent was also a family friend who informed his mother about the scene at the customs office. His mother was quite upset with Paddy. She took a decision to look for a bride through a traditional matrimonial system. The sales at his shop were going down. Bad news was raining on Paddy. Any attempt to meet Padmalaxmi would land him in jail. He was cornered.

Paddy finally decided to quit business and started looking for a job as a Chemical Engineer. He started visiting HR agencies. It was a difficult situation because most of the fresh recruitments had already been made through campus placements. Paddy did not have much of experience and therefore his application could not get through in the mid-level category.

Three old employees had resigned from the shop which was now a mess. Suresh was destroying what had taken Paddy's father two decades to create and build. His mother now visited the shop on a daily basis. She also took charge of the house. Paddy was sitting at home thinking what to do about his life. Going back to Brisbane was an obvious choice, but leaving his mother alone was the difficulty. His heart was breaking into pieces. He was almost in tears when the phone rang.

"Hi mate, how you doing?" It was Mark. Paddy was happy to get a call from his old boss. He spoke to Mark at length. They both discussed the entire situation.

"Why am I failing all the time Mark, why is life so cruel to me?" asked Paddy.

"Because mate, you are not doing what you are good at. All of us have a core competency. It is something that we are naturally good at, something that we do without effort. All you need to do is to recognize your key strengths. Just do what you're good at and life will smile at you" said Mark.

"I am a chemical engineer with an MBA," said Paddy and Mark stopped him from talking any further.

"Mate, you are a born shopkeeper. You rock as a shopkeeper. Your customer management is far above average. The blokes who come to my shop still keep asking for you. Just go back to your shop and take charge. Just do what you are good at and things will start to fall in place. I am sure that you will do very well." Mark's advice was impeccable. Paddy broke through his shell of grief and went to his shop. The staff was shocked on seeing him here after so many years. His mother was delighted.

On the first day, Paddy asked Suresh to purchase more stocks as the shelves were getting empty. He then called the three old employees who had quit. All the three had the same feedback. Suresh was dishonest and was gobbling up the cash. Paddy looked at the accounts. It was true. Suresh had taken undue advantage of his freedom.

"You should hand him over to the police!" said his mother. But Paddy knew that it would cause further damage to the already tarnished image of the shop. He summoned Suresh and sacked him. The three ex-employees who had quit were reinstated. He called for a "come-back" sale. This was a non-seasonal sale that gave a pleasant surprise to his customers. The Padhmanabans were back in business. Sales started picking up slowly but steadily. Life was slowly coming back to normal.

Paddy was now spending more than 14 hours a day in the shop. He was a magnet to his customers. They consulted him before taking decisions. Paddy had a natural flair for being able to quickly understand their needs. He made perfect recommendations or sometimes asked them to wait till new stocks arrived. "Ask Me For Help" batches were given to senior employees and supervisors. His father's dream was coming true.

Within three months, Paddy brought the shop back to its earlier glory. He had now plans to open his second shop. The investors, keen to invest, had all lined up. The meeting was fixed on Saturday morning at 10.00. Paddy had done a lot of homework before this meeting with the investors. He stayed back all night on Friday.

It was 8.00 am on Saturday. Paddy quickly gobbled his breakfast and gathered up all his files. He was about to leave for the shop when his mother stopped him at the door.

"You're coming with me!" she said.

"But Amma, I have a very important meeting and don't have time for the temple now," said Paddy.

"We are not going to the temple. The investors can wait. This is important and needs to be done before I die," she said emotionally.

They sat in the car. The driver knew where to go. Paddy was clueless about what was happening till they entered a house. Paddy's mother had arranged for a match-making session. The girl's parents welcomed them into their house. Coffee and snacks were brought to the table. Paddy was upset with his mother for arranging this unwanted meeting when he was just about to make a big leap toward his second shop. The girl's mother offered them coffee. Paddy lost his cool and stood up.

"Madam and sir, I am sorry for this trouble. But I do not want to marry any other girl. I am already in love with a girl I had met in the customs office. She hates me for sure but I cannot help it. I will marry only that girl. Sorry again. Let us go mom. He walked towards the door. His mother pretended to be humiliated.

"Paddy, please stop, just listen to me!" said his mother.

"Stop it Amma, there are certain things that I will not compromise. If she does not marry me, I will stay unmarried my whole life!" said Paddy as he opened the main door of their house.

"Stop!" It was a voice from behind the curtain "Stop, or I will issue another show cause notice!"

Paddy turned back. It was Padmalaxmi, the girl he had seen at the customs office. They all started laughing. Paddy's dream had come true. He could not believe his eyes. Yes it was her, looking stunningly pretty. She walked up to Paddy and gave him a smile that melted Paddy.

Like what Mark had said, just do what you are good at and things will start to fall into place.

When the agent told Paddy's mom about the customs incident, she realised that Padmalaxmi was the daughter of a dear friend, who had approached her earlier with a proposal for Paddy. But she was not sure if Paddy would return. However with the customs episode, she had directly approached them.

The desired destinations were not far away for Paddy who had now boarded the right train.

Have you boarded the right train ???

Notes

Still Good,,,,,.

"Either quit your part time MBA or submit your resignation" announced the HR manager. Shyam was shocked to hear this. The HR manager could see a question mark on Shyam's face but continued, "Our company has been funding many employees who do part-time MBA while working with us. It was considered as an employee benefit policy that would also work out well for the company. With good management related education in their employees, the company would improve its own productivity" said the HR manager.

"So why this sudden and harsh change?" asked Shyam.

"Well, it has been observed that employees use it as an excuse to leave early from work. On finishing the course, they claim the fees and quit our company. This leads to low productivity levels during their study and waste of company funds when they resign. So the company has taken a tough decision not only to stop this employee-benefit program but also to discourage such activity with immediate effect," he explained to Shyam.

"Sir, I think it is not a fair decision. There could be other reasons due to which employees are quitting. We should work on finding out the exact reasons for attrition." Shyam tried his best but the HR manager was helpless. The decision had come from above. He was only implementing it.

"Let me know your decision by tomorrow" he said before going back to his office.

Shyam was pursuing a part time Master's in Management, a 3 year course with 6 semesters. Shyam had already cleared 3 semesters successfully. He was exactly in the middle of getting a Master's. He was also doing well in his job. The news was disturbing. Shyam started to think about his situation.

"Still good, they have paid me a year's college fees" he said to himself.

He analysed that there were only three options he could consider to move ahead. The first would be to quit the course, the second to quit the job and the third, to cheat them by falsely declaring that he was quitting the course. Most employees in a similar situation opted for the sly third option of a false declaration. But Shyam was honest. He knew that getting a job was not very difficult and a Master's degree was really important for his career. So he boldly informed HR that he wasn't willing to give up college and was ready to resign.

Shyam was a good performer and replacing him would require time. He was asked to look for a job. He was also allowed to work for a few months till he got a new job.

"Still good, I will at least get paid till my next job and they may change their mind if I perform better." No matter what, Shyam was positive.

Monday morning, he reached the office only to see his boss eagerly waiting to discuss a critical matter.

"Shyam, I understand that what happened was unfortunate. I appreciate your honesty. However you can still consider other options," said Sultan, his immediate boss.

"But boss, I can't leave half way" said Shyam.

"Look, I am not asking you to stop the course, but you can always delay it. You could skip a semester. I am sure that this draconian law will not last more than a few months. Once the policy is modified you can re-start your study" Sultan's advice carried logic.

Shyam did not agree with Sultan. He knew that part-time education was difficult and a break would make him lethargic. The inertia in starting it again would be very high. He started looking for a job. He knew that without a new job in the next three months, he would have to stay home without a salary. Considering his hand to mouth situation, this would be disastorous.

Shyam's life had always been full of difficulties. At eleven, he had lost his mother. His father suffered losses in their business. They had to move from one house to another many times. His best friend had died in a bomb blast. They had relatives constantly fighting over disputed property. His grandmother had been bedridden for 5 years. Shyam had lost many good things in life, but the only thing that he hadn't lost was hope. There was some strange power within him that accepted every difficulty and he could convince himself that he was in a better situation. This was the power of positivity. It was such a strong attitude that sorrow or difficulty of any kind could be easily overcome.

"Why do you want to quit your current job?" was the question asked by Freddy, the HR manager of Superx, a European company relatively new to India. Shyam told him the truth. Freddy was impressed by Shyam's optimistic decision to accept the inevitable and not try to exploit loopholes of the system.

"Can a team with a bad leader perform and deliver great results?" was Freddy's next question.

"Yes it can. Provided it has subordinates who have leadership qualities. They would manage the boss and still guide the team toward success" replied Shyam.

"You are hired," said Freddy. Shyam was really happy to get a new job and would also get to hold on to part-time education. Another reason for his happiness was that Freddy had not negotiated on the package. The appointment letter had the right figures, giving him a 40% jump over his current salary. He put in his resignation and joined the new firm. He wore a brand-new white shirt that day. It was his first day in the new office. The traffic was very bad. Still good, I have started quite early to reach my office on time, he thought.

Superx Industries was a European multinational selling large computerised metal cutting machines. All machines were imported. He had joined the Indian office as Sales Manager. His boss headed the Indian operations. The office did not have a very large staff but the number was sufficient to take care of the business in India.

He was introduced to Rati, Satish and Aamir. Rati was a young girl who worked as the secretary to the boss. She was the prettiest girl he had ever seen. Shyam could not believe that there could ever be such a piece of work made by the Almighty. 'She is at a very high level, I am not capable of getting her' thought Shyam 'pretty girls are like difficult sales targets, no point in running to achieve a target that is impossible to attain'.

Satish and Aamir were his senior colleagues in Sales. The first meeting with his new colleagues was pretty cold. It was the first sign of an unhappy organisation. Freddy was a little late that day and immediately took Shyam to Narayan's office. Narayan was the boss. He was in his mid-fifties. He was fat and quite rough with his words.

"Look, we are a no-nonsense company and we do not entertain unnecessary absenteeism. No excuses work on me. I am very strict with the daily reporting and you will not miss a single day" were Narayan's first instructions to Shyam.

'A totally negative boss, although still good, he appears to be going to retire soon. A few years of patience and all would work out well,' thought Shyam. On his first day, he started gathering information on the company and its products. The company provided lunch at the office - more than he had hoped for. Everything else about the company was good. It was a dream company to work for but the only spoke in the wheel was the irascible boss.

That afternoon, he saw Rati crying. He was about to ask her when Aamir stopped him.

"This is common - it happens all the time," Aamir insisted, "she also hates him."

By the end of the week Shyam understood that there was a serious issue in the office. Narayan was a bad boss. Everybody was unhappy. All of them only wanted to retain their jobs, and were just pushing themselves when at work. Nobody tried to make extra efforts. It was a tense situation. A Job Search took place every afternoon including lunch time. Shyam was beginning to feel suffocated. He decided to discuss this with Freddy. 'Still good,- Rati looks amazing even when she cries," he thought pulled to her because of her personality.

"Why do you think I hired you and offered the package that you desired?" was Freddy's immediate query.

"I am discussing a different problem Freddy. It is about Narayan. You need to talk to him. We are on the point of collapsing," explained Shyam.

"Narayan is the blue-eyed boy of Ryan, our company's global Sales Head. We have tried to talk to him and solve this issue. The result was a miserable failure. Narayan only got more abrasive than before. We do good business and our sales figures are excellent. Ryan strongly believes that Narayan's tough approach is highly conducive to the good sales performance of the company."

"Your reply about leadership of subordinates was the reason that we hired you. We were looking for guys who can solve our problem. I am trying to get employees like you in the organisation, so that we can survive. Your psychometric test results displayed very strong leadership skills and the capacity to take on difficult challenges. I have hopes that you will be able to do it." Freddy was serious.

'You have lost it, Freddy. You want to hire 30 year old boys to solve problems that can't be solved by 40 year old experienced players. I will have to burn in this hell for about two years and then move out. Still good, the salary is attractive enough,' thought Shyam.

Every morning a meeting with Narayan was negative. He yelled at and abused every employee for every possible reason. Most of the time Rati used to be seen crying at the table. That was probably the reason she did not wear any make up. But she still looked very pretty. Shyam also was humiliated a few times over trivial issues. 'Still good, only two years left for him to retire,' he thought. Shyam kept pushing himself, absorbing the stress.

Marriage was on the cards for Shyam and he used to spend his weekends looking at girls who came through local match-making agents. In one such meeting, he met Swati, a nice girl of his own caste. During their first date, she asked if he had any plans to do business. Her father was into manufacturing of switches. She was the only daughter and her father wanted a well-educated son-in-law, who would take his business forward. Shyam liked Swati and decided to say "yes" to her question. A few dates with Swati and he was confident they would get married. Their parents met over a meal and fixed a date for their engagement. It was a happy moment in Shyam's life and his fear of Narayan was now at zero level. He was also sure he would resign after marriage. At times, one part of your life helps you with a solution towards another.

"Boss, why are you always upset with me? Why are you always in a foul mood?" "Why do you keep yelling at us?" It was a bold question from Shyam on a Monday morning when all others had left. He was alone with Narayan in his cabin. Narayan was shocked to hear such words from a subordinate. Nobody had ever spoken to him in this tone.

"How dare you ask me such questions? You are insulting me as your boss!" he gave a rude reply.

When you have nothing to fear, courage increases. Shyam took a seat and put his hands on the table.

"I am not insulting you. It is for your own good. Continuous stress and being over-weight can lead to a heart attack. I am sure that your family loves you a lot. At least think about them," said Shyam.

As Shyam completed his sentence, something strange happened. Something which had never happened before and it shocked Shyam. Narayan's face froze and he was immediately quiet with a deathly silence. He did not say a single word. Shyam sat still and did not speak for a minute. Then Narayan got up from his seat, picked up his bag and left the office. He did not say anything before leaving from the office. Shyam had mixed feelings of guilt and curiosity. He decided to follow Narayan secretly. He rushed out from the office to see where Narayan was going.

Narayan reached the parking lot and drove his car out into the main road. Shyam hired a taxi, asking the driver to follow Narayan's car. Shyam desperately wanted to find out why Narayan had reacted in such a manner. Narayan was driving slowly. He drove for about 15 minutes to reach the beach.

He then parked the car. It was about 11.00 am on a Monday morning and the place was quite empty. Narayan walked in the sands to a palm tree and then sat down in its shade, continuously staring at the sea. Shyam stood about 200 meters behind him, closely observing Narayan. The coconut vendor nearby offered a coconut to Narayan. He took it and paid the vendor. Shyam realised that the coconut vendor had done this without being instructed. Shyam went and purchased a coconut for himself. Sipping the coconut's water Shyam kept staring at Narayan.

"He's probably a mad man," said the coconut vendor.

"What? Who?" Shyam was a little surprised to see the vendor react to his observations.

"The man you are staring at," said the vendor, "he comes to this spot very often and sits for 5 to 6 hours. He does nothing but keeps staring at the sea. I am happy because every time he comes, I get good business."

"Strange person" said Shyam, "how frequently does he come?"

"He comes Friday evenings, but I am surprised to see him on a Monday morning," said the vendor.

The vendor did not have any other information on Narayan. However it was confirmed that Narayan came to the beach every Friday evening. Shyam left the beach and got back to the office. He had a lot of work to be finished before Tuesday morning for Narayan's next review. That evening, he asked Freddy to meet him.

Shyam described the whole episode to Freddy who was also shocked on Narayan's reaction and was also pleasantly surprised to see Shyam's bravery at trying to counter Narayan's reign of terror.

"I just cannot believe it" he said, "Narayan remained silent when you argued with him?"

"Look Freddy, the point is that Narayan has some very serious issues. We must investigate the whole matter. It is very important that we understand why he behaves rudely with us," said Shyam, "if we can solve Narayan's problem, he may become less irascible and then all of us can be happy."

"Narayan can remain silent?" Freddy was so shocked that he couldn't accept the truth of the occurrence.

Shyam pushed Freddy to show him Narayan's personal file but Freddy refused. As a professional HR, it would be highly unethical to show any employee's personal file to another. He also requested Shyam to never make such a request again.

During week days, Shyam used to call up Swati after dinner and both of them spoke at length. That evening, Swati seemed a little disturbed on the phone and didn't speak much. She was probably tired. Her family wanted Shyam's exact time of birth. They wanted to calculate the correct and auspicious time for the marriage ceremonies and rituals.

In the next morning's meeting, Narayan was more abusive. His mouth had become an automatic assault rifle, shooting sprays of harsh words. Shyam's report was not complete due to the serious work he had done relating to the investigation. This gave Narayan an opportunity. He did not mince words and attacked Shyam relentlessly. The entire staff kept staring at Shyam, who wasn't disturbed at all. He knew that Narayan was mentally affected and he himself was going to be in the office only for a few days before getting married to Swati. His cool "I don't care" looks further disturbed Narayan. He was now yelling above acceptable decibel limits.

"I will try to do the best I can." It was Shyam who finished the last line. He had a smile on his face as he left the meeting-room. They were all surprised to see Shyam's attitude. The coffee-vending machine was the next halt to calm their nerves.

"You are so cool" said Rati "how can you be so undisturbed?"

"Look guys, nobody can mentally assault you without your cooperation," replied Shyam.

"What do you mean?" Aamir asked.

"You see when Narayan is abusing you or calling you a useless person, your brain is registering this information; it is accepting the abuse and sending a message that the offence is welcome. You believe in the crap he gives you and feel unhappy about it. Basically you are cooperating with Narayan to ensure that you get hurt and feel disturbed," said Shyam.

There was silence for a minute. They were all thinking about what Shyam had just said. He was right, all they had to do was to remain indifferent to Narayan's abuse and not let it affect their mind and heart. After all, Narayan's assault was only mental. A deaf ear to his tirades was all they needed to keep cool and remain happy.

"Look guys," said Shyam, "Keep cool but ensure your performance is not lowered. Narayan cannot throw us out for good performances and all he can do is bark like a mad dog. Still good, we all work for an excellent company. All we need to do is help each other and work like a team with no leader."

"This guy is a guru!" said Satish "O Lord and Guru, tell us something more. Please help us overcome this grief!"

They all had a laugh when Freddy entered the pantry. He was glad to see the office staff having a laugh. This was probably the first laugh he was witness to in the Superx office. It was a moment of joy for Freddy. His decision of hiring Shyam was paying off. It was now important for him to support Shyam.

Freddy, after some reluctance, showed him Narayan's file. Narayan was well educated and highly qualified with degrees from premier institutes of India. He was also a gold medallist at university level. He was 56 years old and had worked in 3 companies before joining Superx. His family record was empty. He hadn't filled in information on his wife and children.

Shyam made a note of Narayan's residential address for further investigation. There was something about Narayan's family that was bothering him. If they could resolve such an issue, life would become happy and comfortable for them all.

That evening as Shyam was about to leave from his office, he saw Freddy waiting for him in the lobby.

"So what do you think should be our next action?" asked Freddy.

"We need somebody who can tell us about Narayan's past," said Shyam

"Better do it fast because you have very little time left," Freddy was a little disturbed, "Narayan has already started to dig your grave. He's put in a bad remark about you to Ryan and recommended dismissing you after a short observation period."

Shyam was least bothered about being fired and wanted to do a good job before moving on to Swati's business post marriage.

Late in the night, he received Swati's call. She was almost in tears and unable to speak coherently. She asked him to meet her the next day before going to work. Shyam had a sleepless night. 'Why can't girls talk sensibly and come straight to the point? Why are they so mysterious?' he thought as he tossed in bed.

At 8.30 in the morning they met at the local park Filled with people walking and jogging. Swati's eyes were red. She probably had not slept the whole night. He went to hold her hand, but she pulled it back and sat sullenly on the bench.

"I have very bad news for you," she started talking with tears rolling down her swollen red eyes, "my elder sister who stays in America has decided to divorce her second husband."

"You mean it is her second divorce and you were crying the whole night for her?" Shyam was getting irritated.

"Well yes, it is her second divorce, but that's not the reason for me to get upset," she continued, "during her first divorce, our family priest had predicted that she would get divorced because the horoscopes did not match. But she had not agreed with our family priest and had then got married to the person she loved. The guy was a big fraud and her marriage collapsed in a few months. After this incident, she avoided remarrying for four years. Then she married her colleague who used to be with her all the time. They understood each other and finally decided to get married. Our family priest once again predicted an unhappy marriage. For the second time he was proved right. My sister is totally broken and my parents are unable to see her suffer."

"Okay, I understand, we can surely delay our marriage till things cool off," said Shyam.

"You haven't understood the situation Shyam!" she was now sobbing loudly. A few joggers stopped and asked whether she needed help. They suspected that Shyam was probably trying to molest her and she had to clarify to them it wasn't so.

"The same priest has predicted a disaster if we get married. We prepared your horoscope from the date and time of your birth. Then, it was compared with mine. Our horoscopes do not match at all!" she finally let the cat out of the bag.

"What nonsense! Are you joking?" was Shyam's reaction "I don't believe in this hocus pocus. What happened with your sister is sheer coincidence. We will be all right, I will prove him wrong. We can also counsel your sister. I can manage it all."

"It is over, Shyam. I cannot afford to put my parents in more grief. They have had enough. If we get married, they will not be able to sleep peacefully. They are not strong enough to see both their daughters in a mess," she was firm on the last line.

For the next twenty minutes, Shyam used all his marketing skills to convince her to marry him. But Swati was resolute in her decision. She gave him a final look, wiped her tears and walked out of his life without even saying goodbye.

Shyam kept sitting on the bench. It took him some time to realise that he was in deep trouble. With the cancellation of his proposed marriage it would also be the end of the business proposal with Swati's father. On the other front, he had taken the highest risk in his job and there was the probability of being fired. It was a classic situation with trouble in all its ramifications.

'Still good, this happened before the marriage and now I have some time left to save my job,' thought Shyam.

"Good morning Freddy!" Shyam was late for work "I have decided to quit my investigation and protect my job. I need the money and getting fired will put me into a serious financial difficulty".

"What, what happened so suddenly that you've lost courage?" Freddy looked worried.

"I need the job Freddy," said Shyam.

"Well, Shyam, you are now in the middle of a maze with very little time left for 'game over'. The finish and start gates are equidistant. If you decide to go back, the maze remains unsolved. So better to fight and finish!" was Freddy's advice.

Shyam was in a confused state of mind as he settled at his desk and switched his computer on. The first email was from Narayan warning him for coming late and not attending a very important meeting. A copy was marked to Ryan and it was a well drafted, grave note. Freddy was right, Shyam had very little time left.

Superx was in the business of selling and servicing heavy production machines. Their bulk sales came from new projects where organisations set up new manufacturing units. The sales representative at Superx would study the project and provide an end-to-end solution with multiple machines and handling equipment. The other orders would include the replacement machines, but these were very small orders. Each year the commerce chamber would issue a list of such new grass-root projects. The names of the companies would become the key prospects for Superx. It was Narayan's responsibility to distribute these prospects amongst the sales team. The list included some companies, mostly multinationals, and those were easy prospects. The machines made by Superx were sophisticated and expensive. Therefore the probability of getting bulk orders from multinationals was high. The list also included some medium scale Indian companies that usually purchased low end machines and avoided automation. Each year, Superx would divide the list fairly and give each sales person some easy multinationals and difficult mid-sized Indian prospects.

It was the same time when Narayan was preparing the grounds to have Shyam sacked and a fresh list of projects had arrived. This gave Narayan a golden opportunity to make a lethal move against Shyam. He personally hand-picked a few companies where chances of getting an order were almost nil. All these companies were added to Shyam's basket. Aamir and Satish ended up getting the cream of multinationals and easier targets. In the next six months, the sales figures would certainly reflect excellent performances by Aamir and Satish. Shyam would be at the bottom, making it easy for Narayan to fire him.

The meeting was cold. The distribution was done by Narayan. He was expecting Shyam to argue or protest. Satish, Aamir and Rati looked at Shyam expecting him to say something. Shyam did not react at all. He simply accepted the list of prospects that were given to him and signed the performance appraisal sheets with all those low probability targets. After the meeting they had lunch in the common pantry area. Narayan always had lunch in his cabin and nobody had ever seen what he used to have for lunch. Satish and Aamir were beginning to feel sad for Shyam.

"We are sorry for what happened to you, Shyam," it was Satish who opened the conversation.

"I suggest that you start looking for a job," said Aamir, "the list of prospects that you have received will lead to zero performance. They are the companies infamous for purchasing only the cheapest machines through the process of tendering. You can get an Order only if you are the lowest on price. Our machines are expensive and you will never be able to compete with local competitors."

"I fully agree with Aamir," said Satish, "my dear, you have boarded a burning train with failed brakes, and your family are passengers on it. So it will be either death by fire or impact. But death is sure for everyone on the train."

Shyam was silent for a long time. He had a smile on his face. Rati kept a hand on his shoulder. She wanted to console him and thought that Shyam might burst into tears.

"What if I can douse the fire and stop the train!" Even now Shyam was able to flash a smile of confidence.

"Shyam, this game is impossible for you to win!" said Rati.

"Rati, I play only those games that seem impossible to be won!" said Shyam. His shoulder was happy to feel the touch of her hand.

"What are you talking about?" asked Freddy who was also on the same table listening to the conversation.

"You see guys my list is weak but long. I have 35 prospects and you guys have just 5 and 7 companies. Therefore my chances are difficult, but better. Secondly, Ryan is not a fool, he will surely understand, based on my list that Narayan is not playing fair. So what Narayan has done can also go against him." explained Shyam.

"Yes, you are absolutely right," jumped Freddy, "Ryan is a firm believer of fair business practices. He is planning to visit us next month. I am sure he will ask Narayan about this unfair list."

"You are awesome Shyam" said Rati "and you were absolutely right with your logic of not cooperating with your mental assaulter. I suffer a little less nowadays."

Shyam's popularity was infectious. The team was impressed by his problem-handling and leadership qualities. They had all started helping each other. Cooperation had increased in the team.

The next three weeks, Shyam worked very hard and did a comprehensive study of those 35 companies. He had a first round of discussions with all their key employees. Shyam was taking notes and tried to understand their problems. He analysed his notes and studied their answers carefully. Shyam also understood that it was an untapped segment. Nobody from Superx had ever approached those companies. He experienced a pleasantly warm welcome particularly from 7 companies who were glad to see Superx approaching them. They were delighted to meet Shyam and discuss the problems they faced. They also allowed Shyam to inspect their shop-floors and make observations regarding low cost machines.

"Can you conduct a time-study for us?" requested the General Manager of MSW, a mid-sized, upcoming auto ancillary company, planning a major expansion project. His name was Sunil and he was the son of the chairman of the company. Sunil was young, dynamic and had just returned home after completing Master's from the US. This was a golden opportunity for Shyam. He had succeeded in his first big step and was sure to prove that the company would require better machines. Once this was done, they would probably give him the opportunity of sending them a quotation.

He came back to the office with a lot of hope and prepared a format for undertaking the time-study. He would also need the technical staff's help. It was a three day project and would require Narayan's approval. Shyam wrote an email to him for approval. Narayan was smart to understand that Shyam had done something that had never been done before. He knew this action of Shyam's was the right investment. But his mind was full of hate. Narayan replied saying that the time-study would be okay, but only on a chargeable basis.

Shyam had expected a negative reaction from Narayan and was preparing his next action plan. Rati had access to all emails that Narayan sent or received. She too was upset with Narayan's decision. Rati had been in the company for a long time. She had had good relations with the technical team's members. She often helped them by protecting them from Narayan's rage. She would sometimes also give them a call when Narayan would be in a good mood and that helped them get their bills signed.

"I can help you Shyam," she called and talking softly on the intercom said, "Please meet me after work in the canteen." Shyam was excited to meet her after working hours.

Rati had convinced two service engineers to conduct a time-study for Shyam on a weekend. They would work two shifts - one on Saturday and the second on Sunday. With four shifts, they would be able to complete the study. Shyam jumped with joy hearing of Rati's support. He immediately called Sunil and confirmed their decision conducting the time-study.

The three boys worked hard during the weekend. Shyam had to spend his own money to buy lunch and dinner for them. He also bought ice-creams to keep them engaged. The study was completed and Shyam presented it to Sunil on Monday. Sunil was impressed by the speed with which Superx had acted. He liked Shyam who was making strenuous efforts for MSW. Generally big brands do not spend a lot of time on small customers. A Mercedes salesman will not even get up from his seat when a common man visits the showroom. Sunil was enjoying the attention he was getting from Superx.

He decided to act fast and sent an official enquiry to Shyam giving him all the future project's details.

The entire team at Superx was thrilled to see the first enquiry of the season come from Shyam. Narayan was also shocked to see the enquiry. But his real shock came when he received a call from Ryan.

"Good morning Narayan" said Ryan "I am happy to see that one of your boys has managed to get an enquiry from a customer who was not our prospect. It is a good opportunity to enter the sector we've never considered before. I am coming down to India for a review and would like to know more. I am also sanctioning a very special price for MSW, because it will open lower-end sector companies. With a bigger population of machines, we will also earn more revenue through services."

Narayan's face became red with anger. In Superx, each enquiry was reviewed by Narayan before uploading it into the common server. Ryan had access to the common server and had seen the enquiry. The inquiry however had been uploaded without his permission. It was done last evening at 21.00 hrs. Only two persons in the company had access to the server for uploading on it, Rati and Ryan himself. He immediately called Freddy and asked him to prepare Rati's termination notice on grounds of insubordination.

"As per company policy, we can terminate only after an official enquiry and the decision would have to be taken by a committee including you and Ryan" Freddy was shaking in fear, "so, I will prepare a communication inviting you and Ryan for a conference call on Rati."

Narayan realised that this action would go against him and he asked Freddy to forget it. He called Rati and fired her for her action. In the history of Superx, it was the first time when Rati came out of Narayan's cabin with a smile on her face. She had taken Shyam's advice on mental assault seriously. She was now happier and more stable to be able to think on her feet.

This information was also passed on to Shyam. The office had become a battlefield just like David and Goliath. Shyam could feel this undercurrent and thought that it was just not right to fuel an internal war at the cost of business. After all, it was the business which had till now given all of them their salary.

Satish and Aamir had more experience than Shyam in making proposals. He took their help when preparing a comprehensive proposal. The offer was good because of the special prices emailed directly by Ryan. A five year owning and operating cost was projected with sufficient margins. Shyam also included another document with recommendations for their existing plant based on the time-study. This was an extra topping to make the deal sweeter.

Sunil's facial expressions clearly indicated that he had liked the proposal. But his eyes were searching for somebody senior. In huge deals, it is understood that a senior appears sooner than later on the scene. Shyam wanted help but knew that Narayan would refuse. Still it was good that Ryan would be coming. He checked with Rati and got the dates when Ryan would be travelling to India. He made a special request to Sunil for advancing the date of final negotiations by a week. Shyam had a plan, a real good plan.

Ryan arrived in India and was welcomed to the office by Rati in traditional Indian style. Ryan always enjoyed the special attention that India showered on him as compared to other countries. He had a one-on-one meeting with Narayan before sitting with the team for an annual review. Shyam, Aamir and Satish prepared themselves to impress Ryan. The three of them having rallied together had formed themselves into a good team. The presentations began with Ryan talking about Superx's global plans and the financial aspects. He announced that India and China would be on the radar. Satish was the first to make a presentation. He had done an excellent job. Ryan was impressed. Even Aamir's work was far above average. Narayan added up the total expected business figures from both of them and passed a note to Ryan.

The last person to make a presentation was Shyam. His first slide spoke about the penetration strategy in India for the new sector. It was a clear indication that he had been given a special job.

"Narayan, this is a tough sector and probably difficult to break. Why have you given this job to Shyam the most junior member in the team?" Ryan's question hit the bull's eye. The entire team was waiting for Ryan to attack Narayan. Their hatred for Narayan was at its peak and they wanted to see him struggle with the question. Narayan paused and cleared his throat to answer. But Shyam stopped him and moved closer to Ryan's chair.

"Please allow me to answer this question sir" said Shyam "This is a joint decision taken by the team. We had a clear list of new expansion projects by different companies. The list was divided into prospects and suspects. In our team, we have two senior and talented sales persons, Satish and Aamir, who were given the task to secure these sure-shot prospect companies. Then we had to decide on the other companies who were suspects and usually purchase cheaper machines. It was decided that I make an attempt to penetrate this market along with Narayan's support. By this decision, we secured our regular business and are also trying to grab some share of the segment that is difficult."

Shyam's statement elicited mixed reactions. Narayan felt guilty. He had done this to destroy Shyam whereas Shyam was trying to protect him. Shyam was also declaring Narayan to be the hero of the team. Rati wanted to break the glass of water on Shyam's head. Satish and Aamir felt totally betrayed. Ryan was cool. He was happy to see a positive answer from Shyam.

"Excellent plan," said Ryan "How do we do it?"

145

"Both Narayan and I feel you should attend the final negotiations meeting with us at MSW tomorrow" said Shyam.

"No problem, Narayan, Let us do this," said Ryan. Narayan fumbled and having no words because of Shyam's attitude, could only nod.

"Sir we were also thinking about conducting a technical seminar for all the companies in my list so that we can give them a chance to discuss issues in an organised debate. This expenditure would certainly help us get more enquires" Shyam had floored Narayan by making him a hero. Now the entire floor belonged to him. Ryan was surprised to see Shyam cooperating with Narayan although Narayan had requested that Shyam be sacked. But he was happy that things were moving in the right direction and the team was together.

Shyam was mobbed by the office-gang during lunch. He was surrounded when Ryan and Narayan were discussing the budget. They accused him of letting a culprit escape without punishment. It was the first chance they had ever had to attack Narayan and it was destroyed by Shyam. Even Freddy was upset and he could not understand why Shyam had turned the tables.

"Look friends," said Shyam, "Narayan is rude but an excellent resource at work, he also might be undergoing some personal issues due to which he behaves in such a manner. Let's forgive him and give him another chance. Remember, if we can change Narayan, we all will have a good boss who would also be a good resource for the company."

"You have a big heart Shyam," said Freddy "but you don't know Narayan, he will never change."

"Freddy, I don't know Narayan; but Narayan too doesn't know me." Shyam had a smile on his face.

Sunil and his father were happy to see Shyam's boss and the global head come for the final meeting. They had an issue with the credit period but Ryan agreed to offer them a special line of credit for one year. The deal was struck. It was Shyam's first order. It was also the company's first order in that sector. Ryan was happy with Shyam. Narayan was still cold with him and didn't speak much. He was however less abrasive toward Shyam now.

The seminar of customers made Shyam's life take a delightful turn. He received 15 more enquires from 28 customers who attended the event. Superx did a presentation featuring MSW. Sunil and his father were the chief guests for the event. In a typical market-related situation, when one does something in a different manner others definitely want to follow.

"You have turned the tables, my friend" it was Freddy who kept his arm on Shyam's shoulder "you have replaced Narayan and are Ryan's new blue-eyed boy. Your job is safe now."

"But Narayan is still the same. If I can change him, the entire office can benefit. Still, it is good that I've entered the safe zone. It gives me the opportunity of playing my next significant move against Narayan," replied Shyam.

"My god, you are dangerous!" Freddy was surprised, "what's the plan?"

"This Friday is Narayan's 56th birthday I want you to plan a surprise party. Invite the whole office. I will be buying a special gift for him," said Shyam secretively.

"Are you mad?" was Rati's reaction when she heard the news of a surprise party for Narayan, "it will happen over my dead body."

"Guys, just relax and trust me. If I succeed, our problems will be over," Shyam was able to cajole them into accepting his decision. They all had started following him.

"Happy Birthday!" they said in a dull voice on entering Narayan's cabin. He was shocked. They were doing it for the first time.

"We don't celebrate birthdays in the office. Let us be professional. Thank you all and now get back to work!" Narayan was serious and stubborn. They were embarrassed and cursed Shyam for getting them into such a stupid situation.

He came forward and said "Sir, we have a very special gift for you. Please give me two minutes; I will be right back with your birthday present."

"Freddy, what the hell is happening? Haven't you told his boy that we do not give gifts in this office?" Narayan was getting back to his original rage. Freddy felt bad about it. He should not have listened to Shyam. He decided to call it off and just before they were about to move out of his cabin, Shyam entered with a large basket covered with a white sheet.

He kept it on Narayan's table and took the white sheet off. The entire team was shocked to see a brown Doberman puppy in the basket.

"Sir, her name is Tubby and she is looking for a good master," said Shyam as he looked Narayan straight in the eye.

Rati was about to scream at Shyam and throw him out of the office. Satish and Aamir thought that Shyam had probably lost his mind due to that small success. Freddy was about to apologize to Narayan for the entire episode. Then a strange thing happened.

Narayan took the puppy in his hand and tears started rolling down his eyes. The entire staff had their mouths open to see this extremely strange situation. In the next 30 seconds, Narayan began to sob like a child. He asked the staff to leave him alone for some time. They all came out of his cabin and stood at the door from where they could hear him weep loudly for a long time. .

Shyam was smiling, they all looked at him. "I can explain," he said as they all stood around to listen to his explanation.

"You see friends," he cleared his throat, "when I was conducting the time study at MSW, I met an old worker in the night shift. I was really tired and had worked continuously for three shifts. He asked me 'why I was making so much of an effort'. My reply to him was that I had a difficult boss and therefore had to work. He asked me the name of my boss and I gave it to him. This old worker happened to be a distant relative of Narayan. That night, I promised him an imported cigarette pack and pressed him to tell me the whole story."

"What story," asked everybody together, "what story?"

"15 years ago, Narayan used to be a jolly fellow. The family consisted of his wife, daughter and his favourite brown female Doberman, Tubby. They were a happy family and Tubby was his darling. Narayan loved Tubby more than his wife and daughter. On an unfortunate Sunday, Narayan took his family to Aksa beach on a picnic. It was his birthday. He decided to celebrate it with the family on the beach. His wife and daughter went for a swim while Narayan and Tubby were relaxing on the beach. Both ladies were excellent swimmers. However Narayan could not swim and he was also afraid of the water. After a few minutes he heard a scream and woke up to see both of them being sucked into the sea. He ran into the water with Tubby, who swam ahead towards them. Narayan shouted for help but there was nobody. Narayan lost all of them. The three bodies were found the next day by the police along with the local fishermen. Everybody was crying at the funeral except Narayan. He did not cry at all. This incident changed Narayan's life. He became stiff and grumpy. The old worker's story gave me an excellent idea to get the old Narayan back. What we saw today was supposed to have happened 15 years ago," Shyam's story had touched everybody.

After about 30 minutes, they all peeped into Narayan's cabin to see him laughing. He was playing with young Tubby. She was wagging her tail with joy.

The entire scenario was transformed at Superx. Narayan became a jolly boss. Shyam managed the highest sale that year from the new sector. Narayan retired after two years making Shyam the chief of the Indian operations.

"Come on Tubby darling, we are late for Shyam and Rati's first wedding anniversary party. Still good, Freddy uncle is here to pick us up." Narayan said as he ran towards the car with the sun setting in the background.

'Laughing and jumping Narayan', 'an incredible Shyam!" thought Freddy with immense pleasure as he connected the Hindi word for 'evening' with Shyam. Freddy picked them up and drove to the party. Their team now because of its Shyam's positivity was going to turn every day's challenge into a party.

Notes

Grand Leader Parents

"I am terribly frustrated in this company with its lousy employees and stinking dirty politics" said Aditya to his colleague and friend Akanksha.

Aditya Kulkarni worked with Acme International, a multinational. He had joined two years ago as a Business Development Executive. The company was a role model for the wrong reasons. It had all types of unfair and unethical practices. Aditya was denied his well-deserved promotion. His sales were good with a strong 30% growth. His colleague, however who had similar achievements and had appointed third party commission agents for all deals had got promoted. This had led to corruption as the agents undertook a number of transactions under the table. In all under-the-table deals efforts by a sales team are almost zero.

Akanksha was a receptionist and friendly with Aditya. Akanksha liked him very much but Aditya did not have special feelings for her although she was quite pretty. Aditya was of the serious and studious type. He treated her like a friend unlike others who viewed her as an object of beauty. She always listened to him with the utmost interest.

Priya's promotion wasn't a mystery. With very low performances and high absenteeism, Aditya was certain that Priya's promotion had been because of her dress-sense. She hardly ever wore anything decent. The boss was always happy to see her in the office. Priya ensured that she spent the maximum amount of time at work with the boss, discussing petty issues. With a voice that was deliberately sweet, she knew how to roll her 'R's. Her friendship was highly limited to the bosses and the HR team. Her stilettos announced her arrival. Being an audio-visual treat she got the highest praise for the most trivial of efforts.

Priya and Aditya were virtual enemies and regularly fought in various meetings over issues. The boss however always deemed Priya to be right. Priya usually made sure that Aditya suffered for talking against her in the meetings. This was probably one of the reasons why he had so far not been promoted.

Aditya could handle it no more and left with Akanksha to join the others for lunch. In the cafeteria the faucets leaked. So he did not have to open a closed faucet to wash his hands. The company offered subsidized lunch for all employees. He took an empty plate to load it with rotis, vegetables, dal etc. While crossing the sink, he saw that there was more food in the used plates than in the one he had just now filled for himself. The company's lunch rules did not allow second helpings. Employees therefore used to overload their plates leading to collosal wastage of food. Nobody in the HR could be bothered to take action against this disturbing wastage of food.

In general, nobody bothered about anything at all and continued to be apathetic. It was all about dragging oneself through the five day week to enjoy the salary and weekends. During lunch, they all were planning the extra-long weekend with a holiday coming up on Friday as well as Monday.

Aditya too needed a break. He decided to visit his paternal grandparents in Kolhapur, a town in southern Maharashtra. Aditya had lived with his grandparents all his life. His parents had died in an accident when he was five years old. His grandfather was a rich businessman. He owned a large sugar factory. The Kulkarni family was one of the oldest and most-respected suppliers of sugar. Tara Sugar Mills, owned by the Kulkarnis was known for the rich quality of sugar. Tara Sugar Mills was the company started by his great grandfather. The business had then been taken over by his grandfather, who was Aditya's great grandfather's step-son, when he was a young boy and his grandfather had made it flourish and expand with his sharp business acumen. Wanting Aditya to experience the real world on completing his education, Aditya's grandfather pushed him to work for a company for a few years before joining the family business.

Thursday afternoon, Aditya bunked work to catch the bus to Kolhapur. He did not bother to inform his boss because he had no intention of returning. He wanted to talk to his grandfather about frustrations at his workplace. He was sure his grandfather would ask him to join the family business immediately.

"Good morning Dada!" Aditya greeted, his grandfather.

"Hello my boy, such a pleasure to see you here!" he was glad to see his grandson. The grandmother was busy using Aditya's favourite recipes to cook. She had never wanted him to leave home to work. She usually asked the servants to cook the base of many dishes but this time she was cooking herself.

"Dada, I have had enough. I want to come back." Aditya said.

"Oh, finally, such a good thing, yes my boy, come back immediately. We are all waiting to have you here," said the grandmother who had just entered the dining room. She came and sat on the table next to him "have you put in your papers?"

"No Aai, I just wanted to inform you and take your permission before putting in my papers," he replied. He called his grandmother "Aai" which means "mother" in Marathi. She had always been a mother to him.

His grandfather did not continue the discussion and his grandmother began pushing food into his mouth.

"We should also look for a good wife for you. I want to see my great grandchild before I die" Aai was now getting all emotional.

Dada had to leave early and left immediately after breakfast. But there was no comment from him. Aditya knew his grandfather very well. He spent the day with Aai. There was a lot to do at home. Dada was back at dinner. Aai had arranged for a traditional family meal with two sweets. After dinner, Aditya looked his grandfather straight in the eye.

"What are you looking at?" Dada asked.

"You did not say anything about my decision. I'm sure something is bothering you," he replied.

"Don't bother about him; he's getting old and whimsical. You simply come back," said Aai.

"No Aai, I want to know what's on his mind," said Aditya, "Dada, tell me the truth!"

"You said that you had had enough," said Dada "Is there something that is bothering you at work?"

Aditya explained to them the situation that existed at his work-place, the politics, the frustrations and the rotten culture. He also told them about his hard work and failure to get promoted. They both listened to him patiently. When Aditya finished they looked at each other. Aai had a sad look on her face. She kept nodding her head and got up from her chair.

"No Aditya, you cannot come back" she said, and Dada nodded his head in agreement.

"But why?" Aditya was shocked at such a reaction.

"We never back out on defeat. The battle has to be fought till victory is obtained," she said.

"What are you talking about?" he asked, "what battle?"

Then it was time for Dada to speak. He put a hand on Aditya's shoulder and said, "Look dear, we don't want losers in our business. It is only for winners. You want to come back because you have lost many battles in the office. We want you to go back, fight and win. Come back when you win, we will welcome you. But if you come after losing, you will keep losing all your life. You will never win at all."

"Look, this isn't about winning or losing, there are no battles, there is no enemy. I am just sick of the system, the culture and therefore want to quit. After all, I belong here, this is my home!" said Aditya.

"This is definitely your home and your business. It all belongs to you. However, I have one question. Would you have come back had you got that promotion? asked Dada severely.

"Well, I might have continued for a year and then returned anyway!" replied Aditya.

"That's just the point! We want you to quit after getting that promotion or making a significant change in and to the organisation!" said Dada.

Aditya pondered over this point. They patiently watched him. They could see the spark on his face gone. He was disturbed over something.

"I am too weak to do it. They are extremely strong. Nobody will support me. I will never have the strength of numbers. The boss knows all the other departments' heads. Priya's contacts are even stronger. They will surely win and then have me thrown out of the organisation within no time," said Aditya.

"Let them be strong, let them be greater in numbers, you can still win," said Aai.

"Listen guys, you don't know what it is all about in the corporate world, you have never been there or done that. In my world, the weak cannot defeat the strong. Actually in any area the weak cannot defeat the strong," argued Aditya.

Both of them had a big smile on their face. As if they knew how to win in the corporate world. Aditya, looking at them smiling, was confused. He knew for sure that they had never worked before and were always involved in the sugar business.

"We come from a royal family of fighters. Our ancestors developed mastery in defeating strong and large armies with small teams of soldiers. I will have to tell you this story narrated to me by my grandfather," said Dada.

"Hello, this has got nothing to do with history or sword-fighting, it is a corporate game. It's completely different" said Aditya.

"I will still want you to hear this story" said Dada.

"Please give me a break - I want to sleep now" said Aditya. He further insisted that "history and the corporate world are two completely different entities."

"Yes they are but both have similar concepts. . And you are a lousy storyteller, let me tell you this story," said Aai "it goes like this:

Many years ago, our ancestors lived near Paithan, in a small village called Mungi, along the banks of the great river Godavari. We were a happy family involved in cotton-farming. We were not very rich but certainly well–to-do. Working in the fields was hard but everybody was involved. Those days there was no television or any other entertainment. The entire family worked in the fields. They also had to protect themselves from wild animals and other enemies. Each harvest season, the farmers picked cotton from the fields and brought the cotton into a common area to press into bales. The traders from Paithan would come to their village and buy the cotton bales. In exchange for the cotton, the traders would pay in gold as well as goods as barter. The villagers worked very hard. The bales of cotton had to be ready in time. Working in the fields was at its peak. But a young girl called Kamla was not to be found in the fields. She wasn't seen to be working. Instead, she was sitting by the banks of the great river Godavari, busy throwing stones into the river. 'I'm sick of working in these fields!" she said loudly while throwing a big stone that splashed into the river. She had lost interest in work a long time ago. Working in the fields was frustrating. She was never made for this work. She was different and ambitious. She had been nursing an ambition even boys of her age wouldn't even dream of. Now 14 and obsessed by her ambition since she was ten, she had decided to become a 'Farzand`. In the 17th century, "Farzand" was a military title, given to a Maratha commander capable of commanding an army of 10,000 or more. It was a very high rank in the army, considered equal to that of a prince.

This ambition was developed due to an incident in her life. The story began when she started going with her father and older brothers to Resula, a neighbouring village to learn new methods of sowing cotton seeds. A couple of families from Mungi used to go every day to Resula and return at sunset. There was a thick forest between the two villages. The forest was infested with wild animals, but the villagers used to be well-prepared. They always walked in groups, with women and children being kept in the middle. Adult males with armed weapons kept a strict watch to ensure the group's safety. There were patches of the forest where senior members became alert on getting a strong smell of a wild animal.

On the last day, the group was a little late while returning. Everybody was happy because the villagers of Resula had given them a superior quality of cotton seeds as a gift. They were chatting and laughing on their way. Just then the youngest child in the group spotted a ripe mango under a tree. He asked Kamla for it but she refused and he dashed out of the group to pick it up. Suddenly a leopard appearing out of nowhere, with lightning speed picked up the boy and vanished into the jungle. The men were shocked. They reacted by running behind him with their weapons. The leopard was amazingly swift and the boy was lost forever.

This scene had occurred in front of Kamla's eyes. While the boy's family suffered, the villagers regretted the sad incident and eventually the episode was forgotten. But Kamla could never forget. She just could not take her mind off the scene. Their group was strong, had weapons and it was simply impossible for any wild animal to have won against them. But the leopard was fast, and was hiding, and must have definitely been observing them for quite some time. He had launched his attack at the right time and moved out before the group could even react. She was amazed to see an individual win against a team by adopting a technique. The leopard's technique consisted of attacking with speed, taking the enemy by surprise, launching only a partial attack and escaping before the enemy could react. Her mind began to work on a unique idea. Kamla was no longer the same as before. She forgot her daily tasks. She started spending more time with the boys who used to practice martial arts. Her parents were happy that she had begun taking an interest in fighting. The villagers generally encouraged the children to learn and practice martial arts for defending themselves against animals or in other violent situations.

Within a few years, Kamla became a master in 'patta-fighting'. A 'patta' is a special type of sword which can be used for defence when you are surrounded by more than two enemies. She was very fast and could easily defeat boys not just of her age but even those older and stronger.

Back at the Godavari river bank, the 14 year old beautiful Kamla just sat with a sad face.

"Kamla, Kamla!" her father called out. "What are you doing? we have a lot of work to be completed, don't just sit around wasting time." She reluctantly got up and followed her father back to work.

"What happened my child, why are you so sad? He asked Kamla.

"I'm not interested in this work, baba!," said Kamla.

"But this is our profession, we are farmers, my dear," said her father.

"I don't want to be a farmer, I want to become a Farzand" she replied.

"O my child, you mustn't dream of the impossible. Come, let's go back to work" her father was genuinely concerned.

It was a good harvest that year and the farmers of Mungi were happy. The traders arrived with lots of goods for barter. They travelled to various villages accompanied by Mavlas, the soldiers. The traders carried expensive goods and needed security. A chunk of their earnings had to be offered directly to the Maratha lord's treasury. Kamla was with her father who had stacked the harvest for traders to check.

Trade began at sunrise and she was rubbing her sleepy eyes when a man entered their stacked area. She was mesmerized by his appearance. He was tall, well built and good looking. He was staring at her. They could not take their eyes off each other. It was love at first sight, both ways. A strange mixed feeling of content, acceptance and love.

"My name is Baji, I am a Maratha Mavla" he introduced himself. Kamla had no focus on the trading that took place. She was busy talking with Baji and both were lost in their own world. The merchants were in the village for two days.

On the third day when they had to leave, Baji appeared at Kamla's house,

"I want to marry your daughter" he said with courage and confidence.

They were all taken by surprise. Kamla was delighted but her face didn't show acceptance or denial. Her parents took her into the house for discussion. They also made enquiries about Baji's family, profession etc. Finding his background satisfactory, they agreed to his proposal.

"I will marry you subject to your agreeing to a condition that I shall always be with you everywhere, in the house and on the battlefield," said Kamla.

It was not an ordinary set of conditions. Her parents were shocked to hear them.. But Baji had a sly smile on his face.

"The battlefield is not a safe place. I will accept your condition only if you are able to defeat me in combat!" he challenged.

What happened ahead was predictable. Kamla chose the patta and surprised Baji with her deft moves. The battle was intense. The observers were delighted to see a combat between two experts. Nobody was sure if Baji had deliberately allowed himself to be defeated or it was Kamla who had actually defeated him.

That winter both families came together for the marriage of Baji and Kamla. It was then time for Kamla to bid farewell to her family and friends. She proceeded with her beloved husband to their new home in Bhataudi, a village near Ahmednagar in Maharashtra.

Romance was in the air. The forest was beautiful. The love-birds enjoyed their bullock cart ride followed by a few friends on horseback. The bullock cart was full of a variety of gifts given by the family and well-wishers.

Newly wedded couples generally talk about themselves or about raising a family. But this couple was different. Their favourite topics were weapons and war strategies. Kamla often spoke to him about her ideas on a series of quick short attacks to disturb the enemy, and she was delighted to find him appreciative.

Baji was posted in Bhataudi by his Maratha lord, the great Shahaji Raje Bhosale. He was in-charge of the camp along with his troop of ten fighters. It was a 14 day journey from Mungi to Bhataudi. The last day of the journey began at sunrise when a rider approached them.. Both drew their swords as a safety measure. It was Kurmu, Baji's assistant and he appeared worried.

"They have seized our village, a hundred of them, and we will have to wait in the forest till they leave," he was upset.

In the 17th century, the Moghuls dominated most parts of the country and moved in groups consisting of a minimum of a hundred soldiers. During a journey they used a village on the way to set up camp. The villagers were either killed or driven away. The houses, cattle, food and water bodies were used by them. After taking rest for a few days, the Moghuls would then move onward and the villagers would eventually return back to their damaged homes with nothing remaining - no food, money or cattle.

Baji agreed to hold a camp in the forest.

"Let us fight and drive them out of our village" said Kamla. Kurmu laughed. It was good to see his gloomy face change.

"They are 100. We are only 10, Vahinisaheb. They will finish us in no time. We are no match for them" said Kurmu. Marathas addressed the wives of their seniors as "Vahinisaheb."

"Call all 10 of your men and get me the minor details. I have a plan" she said.

The entire group of Marathas, the villagers and her lord Baji were amazed to see the way she conducted the discussion. She asked many questions, with an eye for detail. Her acumen was natural and strong. Baji was falling in love with her again and again. He was proud to have married a woman who instantly had been able to command the respect of his entire village. She became "Vahinisaheb" to all of them.

As the sun rose over the Moghul camp in Bhatuadi a few goats were spotted by the soldiers, who rushed and captured them. The army commander Dilshan was delighted to see his men catch seven goats from the forest.

"Let us have a good lunch today men, we have earned it," said Dilshan. If only he knew that those goats had been sacrificed by Vahinisaheb as part of her plan!

That afternoon, after a heavy meal, the Moghul soldiers having become drowsy, were relaxing. They had got a chance to eat their favourite meat after a long time. The silence of the afternoon was broken by cries of a pretty young woman running towards their camp all alone. She was crying.

"Help me, help me, they will kill me," she yelled.

The guards took her to Dilshan. She was still crying. Most of the soldiers had left their post on seeing a beautiful woman enter their camp. Before Dilshan could speak, there was another cry from the north side of the camp. A group of 5 horsemen had attacked, slashing away at any soldier who dared to come in their way. Dilshan was furious, he left the women unattended and started running towards the north side with other men. By the time he reached they had escaped into the forest.

"After them, kill them" he shouted. 15 Moghul cavalry soldiers rushed after them.

In the next two minutes, he heard screams, "Fire, fire, fire" Dilshan heard his soldiers running away as a blast of fire rose high into the air. The women, who had come seeking help was

Vahinisaheb. She had set the main tent on fire. The entire stock of gunpowder and weapons was on fire causing a blast killing a few more men. She then removed her hidden patta, killed some more and mounted a horse to head straight into the forest.

Dilshan was utterly confused. The next thing to happen was a similar five-men attack from the southern side of the camp. They too ventured into the forest after killing a few more Moghuls. The troop of 15 soldiers who had entered the forest never came back because they had entered a trap made of ropes laid to trip the horses and seriously injured the men. It was easy to kill them after this injury.

As the sun set that evening, Dilshan was left with only 20 soldiers. Most of them had died in the fire, surprise attacks or forest traps. Their ammunition was destroyed. Dead bodies were strewn across the camp.

"I swear to Allah that I will not rest till all the Marathas are finished!" shouted Dilshan. They worked hard throughout the night to bury the dead, clear what was left of the weapons and re-arrange the camp.

On the next day, the tired 21 Moghuls met the well-rested and fresh 10 Maratha soldiers being led by a pretty woman riding a horse. It was a straight easy win for the Marathas.

Within 48 hours, 10 Marathas led by a woman had destroyed the entire Moghul battalion of 100 soldiers with ammunition. The news spread like wildfire. Baji's Lord, Shahaji Raje Bhosale, was delighted to hear that 10 Marathas led by a woman, had destroyed the entire 100 male Moghul troop within 48 hours. He sent a personal invitation to Baji and Kamla. Shahaji was impressed by Kamla's ideas. They were asked to assist Shahaji in his battles.

In those days, Shahji's territory was under the Nizam's jurisdiction. He was a young Maratha warlord who called himself "Raje", i.e. 'king' in Marathi.

As time passed, Kamla and Baji took turns in training soldiers in their new technique of high speed ambush attack. It was all about stalking your enemy, laying a trap, waiting in ambush for the right time, imitating birds' calls as signals, launching an attack and then escaping even before the enemy could realize what had happened. They regularly made soldiers exercise running with great speed in difficult terrains of the forest and the hills.

A few more well-thought out victories made Baji and Kamla Shahji's the favourites of everyone. But there was one man who was extremely unhappy with the success of Kamla and Baji, Sharifji - Shahji's brother. Sharifji became terribly jealous because Shahji now no longer took his advice in planning battles. Sharifji saw Kamla as his rival. He saw her as a contender for the post of the army chief. He began to secretly work out a plan to eliminate Kamla.

In those days, Shahji was under the Nizam shahi who was at war with the Moghuls. One evening, on returning to camp, Shahji summoned Kamla and Baji.

"The Mughals and Adilshahi sultanates have joined hands. My master, Malik Amber Sahib wants us to stop them at Bhataudi," he said.

"How large is their army?" asked Kamla.

"With both joining forces, I see that they would have over 200,000 men. Even our guerrilla attack won't work on them. Remember, we also have to protect Ahmednagar," said Shahji.

This time the situation was decidedly quite tough. Kamla needed a new idea. Their battalion had only 20,000 men, of whom they would need a minimum of 10,000 to cover and protect Ahmednagar. Therefore she could use only 10,000 men to defeat an army of 200,000. She was sure that the enemy would have studied her past strategies. They would be prepared to tackle her sudden attacks. They would also attack Ahmednagar to break Shahji's power. That night she and Baji disguised themselves as an old couple and rode into the forest to study the situation themselves.

The army had camped on the bank of the Mehkari river. It was a huge army. They had elephants, canons, horses, an armoury and strong well-built soldiers. A group of men pulling cannons were walking towards them. Kamla and Baji had to quickly hide behind the trees. Suddenly, Kamla and Baji saw a cannon slip falling into a ditch. Six men were unable to pull it out. They then summoned Afzal Khan, a giant of a man. The tall and muscular Afzal Khan single-handedly pulled the cannon out.

As Kamla and Baji returned to their camp Shahji asked them about their observations. Baji told him about Afzal khan and the power of their army.

"I see a defeat" said Shahji, "what do you say Kamla?"

"I am confident that we can win." She had a smile on her face.

"How?" asked both Shahji and Baji.

She remained silent. Shahji asked all the men to wait outside, including Sharifji who took his exclusion to be a big insult. He felt humiliated on being asked to wait outside.

At Shahji's personal chamber, Kamla had prepared a rough drawing which she showed them.

"We have something which is far more powerful than the entire army" said Kamla.

"My lord! The entire army is camping on the river which flows north-south. Before the camp there is a dam. With good rainfall, the dam is now full. If we blow the dam away, the entire army will be submerged under water. We can then attack the remaining of their army that will manage to survive this catastrophe," said Kamla.

"Brilliant" said Shahji and Baji together.

That night, the Mughal and Adil soldiers suddenly woke up to see huge quantities of water gushing into their tents. The dam had blown apart. They started running for their lives. Clothes, rations, arms, ammunitions, cannons, cattle, everything was going down into the water. Dead elephants and horses were seen floating in the water. This catastrophe was followed by a brutal attack from Shahji's troops. The victory was confirmed. Kamla and Baji were in the battlefield. They could capture most of the enemy chiefs as prisoners.

As the battle was coming to an end, they received news that the Moghuls had captured Sharifji. Kamla rushed to save him. She saw Sharifji fighting with the giant warrior Afzal Khan. Kamla rushed to save him with her patta. She moved forward and took him head on. It was her duty to protect Sharifji. Totally focused on Khan's moves she felt excruciating pain in her back. It was Sharifji. He had struck her with a sword from behind. She was bleeding profusely.

"Why?" she questioned him with pain in her eyes. Both looked at each other. At this moment, Afzal khan found the opportunity to rush forward and kill both Kamla and Sharifji.

Baji arrived on the scene to see Afzal Khan killing both. He screamed with pain and attacked Afzal Khan with his sword. Afzal Khan ran into the forest. Baji ran behind him. It was the last time the other Marathas had seen him. They could never trace his body.

The war was won but Kamla and Baji were no more.

"I will never be able to repay her debt. Ensure that her last rites are performed with the status due to a Farzand!" Shahaji instructed his men.

Later, the Adilshahi awarded Shahaji with the title of Farzand. He was continuously thinking about Kamla during the ceremony. It was after all her military intelligence that had got for him this success.

Some wishes take long to get fulfilled, but true leaders ensure that the purpose is achieved. History respects such souls.

Thus ends the story of Kamla, a true leader and an immortal Farzand!!!

"Wow, what an awesome story" said Aditya "I just don't believe it. Is it a true story?"

"Not the story, but the lesson is more important" said Dada "you need to understand that the weak can win against the strong provided they plan the attack in such a way that it works effectively. Think about the weakness of your opponent, make sharp and small attacks. Once he is weak, you can go in for the kill."

"That is the tough part" said Aditya "I need to frame a strategy to lay a trap."

"Let us sleep now - it is getting very late," said Aai, "tomorrow we shall discuss your master strategy."

Aditya was excited and he wanted to do it immediately. But the rule was simple - you have to do the thinking with a fresh mind. Aditya could not fall asleep for a long time. He was thinking about the story. The door flew open, it was Priya. She was dressed in a hot outfit and had a sword in her hand. She pounced on his bed and mercilessly chopped his feet and then threw her sword and grabbed his shoulder. She was trying to pull his hands out from his shoulder-blades.

"Wake up, wake up!" he heard. Aai had come into his room and was waking him up by shaking his shoulder. It was just a bad dream. A horrible dream at dawn. As a child, Aditya had always been told that dreams seen during the dawn come true. He was now really worried. He had a bath and came out into the main hall. The three of them meditated for 20 minutes. Then they had breakfast before starting their discussion. Aditya was asked to start telling them all the things that had happened in his office. He was told not to spare anything. The finest detail had to be informed. Aai was continuously taking notes of what he was saying. Aditya was surprised to see his grandparents acting like consultants. He was also surprised to see his old and less educated grandparents approach a serious issue like professional MBAs.

After a lot of listening, Dada and Aai had a short conversation amongst themselves. Aditya was asked to arrange a cup of tea in the kitchen. Both the local servants have become useless, he thought. They were on holiday since a week and Aai was now managing the entire show. Aditya made the tea himself and sat down with them to continue the discussion.

"Well!" spoke Aai, "it is very clear that we have two enemies in this situation"

"Absolutely correct, it is Priya and my boss Rakesh!" said Aditya.

"Just shut your mouth and listen" Aai was annoyed, "the two enemies are not so prominent. One is an internal enemy and the other is external. It is very important to defeat the internal enemy first. Unless the internal enemy is defeated, the external can never be challenged."

"The internal enemy is your own ego," said Dada "unless we destroy your ego, nothing can be done. You will just keep attacking and continue making mistakes"

"You guys do not understand the corporate game," said Aditya "this has nothing to do with my ego."

"I was sure that you would deny it, this is a standard reaction," said Aai "just answer a simple question: Would your troubles reduce if Priya was your best friend and well wisher?"

"I am not sure," Aditya took a minute to reply "yes, it would. She would not do all that bitching to my boss. I do agree that Priya needs to be eliminated."

"No you fool!" said Aai "Jealously and hate arise out of ego. We must kill it first. You cannot eliminate your corporate enemies. We are not in the 17th century anymore."

"So our first step is to get you in action by making friends with Priya. We have to get her on to your side." It was Dada.

"Impossible! I will not be able to do it. We are established enemies. She will not even talk to me. But why should I make her my friend? This is war." Aditya was upset at the prospect of making friends with a person he hated the most.

"It is just the beginning. You will have to get her to like you. It will clear your path in the war against the entire system. Priya is Shakti, the goddess of strength. When she is with you, victory is assured," said Aai "Imagine what can happen if you and Priya fight together for your promotion. Let us post a target of one year and you getting the promotion. Once you are promoted, just get back to Kolhapur and take charge of our business."

"Your next target is Rakesh, your current boss. But you need to first check if he is corrupt. Remember, when you build your army, never take those who are corrupt or have integrity issues. They will spoil the mission," said Aai.

"Remember your real strength is to avoid getting emotional or getting angry or raising your voice in a meeting. You can only win with a completely ego-free and emotion-free mind-set. This attitude must be coupled with a rock-solid performance. Hard work and sensibility will take you to the top. Ego, anger and other negative emotions will always pull you down." It was Dada advising him now after Aai was through.

When Aditya left his village, he had changed. This visit had created a strong effect. He was now determined to play the game with style. His grandparents had given him fantastic advice. What a great couple they were, he was proud to be their grandson. He was also happy to know that he himself hailed from a family of great warriors. The story of the weak winning against the strong had created an indelible mark on his mind.

It was a Monday morning and the office had dull employees turning up at their work stations. Aditya had a fresh look. He reached his table and switched on his computer. The first email was from Priya. She had written a nasty email about the follow-up done by Aditya in the last sales pitch. She had also accused him of not sending a particular quotation on time. The email had been marked to Rakesh, the product manager, HR and three other sales persons. It was a sharp attack with all efforts being made toward Aditya's humiliation. Under normal circumstances, Aditya would have returned the email giving full details of her not giving him the required estimates and information on time. He would have also mentioned the mistakes she might have made on the estimates, making her look very silly in front of all.

However, Aditya was now a professional warrior. He wrote a stunning reply to Priya. He agreed with all that she had alleged, apologized for his weak performance and praised her for the excellent work. He also requested her support and expert guidance to him in work. This reply delivered a 440 volt shock to Priya. She had never expected this type of reply from Aditya. She did not know how to react. To her it appeared an evil move and she assumed that Aditya might attack her for the mistakes she had made. This did not happen at all. He had already made all the corrections and submitted the proposal to the customer. When they received the order, he sent a thank you email to Priya for her support. This email was marked only to her and Rakesh, their boss. Rakesh forwarded that email to her and his boss. They all sent her an appreciation note. She became the heroine for the order which she had actually messed up. "Sorry" is a very strange power-tool. It works when the fault is yours. However it works extremely well even when the fault is not yours.

In the next two months, Aditya and Priya became the best of friends in the organisation. His first mission successful led to Priya giving loads of information. She knew everything about Rakesh. He was a corrupt man, who made money from the agents and distributors of the company. She also knew about the other heads of departments involved in similar misdeeds. Corruption was rampant in the organisation and the only way out was to cleanse the system by approaching the CEO, Mr. Wilson directly. But this was not possible because he met only the department heads.

Aditya decided to take the risk. His team now consisted of two pretty girls, Akanksha and Priya. This created the required situation to bolster courage. Akanksha was his source of getting the records for retrieving Mr. Wilson's personal email id. On a Friday evening, Aditya sat at his desk to type out his email. He decided to be diplomatic and not write directly. The written message was,

Dear Sir,

With courage and sincerity, I break the rules and directly approach you with a suggestion that I think is in the best interest of the company.

Ethics, environment and culture are parameters that I request you to add into our appraisal system currently based only on "number crunching" and "result orientation".

Ethics is our heart. It plays a very important role while winning orders, taking strategic decisions, selecting suppliers and employees. We should avoid every act such as paying commissions, making false promises on deliverables, creating cartels, adding ambiguous clauses in contracts; arm twisting suppliers, unfair trading and the list is long. These transactions ultimately cause blemishes on our brand and in our work.

The environment is our life, without which we shall cease to exist. A/Cs and lights not switched off after meetings, large quantities of food wasted in the canteen, effluent treatment, leaking taps, use of plastic bags, liberal use of paper, not using natural lighting, motion sensors in toilets and I can keep on adding.

Culture is the soul of the organisation. I have observed verbal abuse, harassment, unfair recommendations, ill treatment meted out to juniors, provocative dressing, racial remarks, gifting superiors, misuse of office infrastructure etc. These generate strong and negative feelings and I have to drag myself to work.

No organisation is perfect, but when performance is backed by ethics, environment and culture, the results are happy employees, eager suppliers, more business and an unblemished brand image, just like a person with a good heart, healthy life and a noble soul.

With these parameters, you will observe that the bar has been raised. Not all current top performers will be able to maintain their status. This is the change we urgently need. I am sure that you will take action or simply inform my superior, leading to my exit. Trust me sir, in both the cases, I am eventually going to emerge the winner.

Regards

Aditya Kulkarni – Employee number 02568.

His hands were shivering as he pressed the 'Send' button. The email was shot, the war had begun. But as days passed, nothing actually happened. Aditya was upset. The CEO probably hadn't read the email. He rechecked with Akanksha the email address. In Priya's opinion, the CEO probably might have taken it as a joke. She always wanted Aditya to write directly about the corrupt bosses. She was known to be aggressive.

Sheetal was the CEO's secretary and Akanksha's friend. Akanksha was also trying to check if she had information. But Aditya had clearly instructed her and Priya not to reveal his secret to anyone. Sheetal was aware that Akanksha, Priya and

Aditya were friends. They usually ate lunch together. Aditya's close contact with two pretty girls was making the men envious. It was another big worry for Aditya because it would indirectly affect his promotion.

One day, Sheetal came to lunch and sat at the same table. She introduced herself to Aditya. The other girls got the hint. They quickly finished their lunch and left the table. Aditya played normal.

"You must apply for the new position that will be announced today, goodbye!" said Sheetal before leaving the lunch room.

Aditya had a smile on his face. The same day, a new position, "Executive Assistant to CEO" was announced on the intranet. The criteria for this position had been created keeping Aditya in mind. His personal file was checked for his qualifications and experience. His profile was a clear fit.

"It is for you, Aditya," said Priya, "it is evident that you will be the selected one."

The position indeed was for Aditya. The interview was just a formality. The CEO selected Aditya as his executive assistant.

Within a year of his appointment, Aditya was able to make significant changes in the ways of working in the organisation. His position gave him the authority to probe people, deals, systems etc. He was able to divide big tasks into small assignments. As the clean-up began, people eventually got the message. Most of them came on track themselves. With active involvement and transparency, a leader can beneficially transform an entire organisation. Even Priya started wearing decent clothes. The CEO was extremely happy with Aditya, who got elevated to a higher grade with a raise in salary. His name was added to the international talent list to be groomed for a role as the head of a unit.

Aditya was now in a dilemma. He had started to love his job but knew his future lay in Kolhapur. His grandparents were happy that he had been groomed for the big role. Dada informed him to keep it on a few more months till he could get fully ready.

"Where are you from Mr. Aditya?" asked the bank manager. Aditya had to visit the bank for checking the papers on behalf of the CEO.

"I am from Kolhapur," replied Aditya.

"What a coincidence, my last posting was Kolhapur," said the Manager, he was a little extra talkative for a bank manager, "are your parents in Kolhapur?"

"Well, we own the Tara Sugar Mills." Aditya replied.

"Oh God, so you are Mr. Aditya Mirchandani?" he asked "So nice to meet you in person."

"What, no, I am Aditya Kulkarni, grandson of Sadashiv Kulkarni, why should I be Mirchandani?" Aditya was puzzled. The bank manager was now sounding very irritating.

"But," the manager took a long pause "I am definitely sure that Tara Sugar is owned by the Mirchandani family. I have met the owner myself. I also know Mr. Sadashiv Kulkarni very well; he works in the same company and manages the entire show. He is a good man and does a fantastic job. He is Mirchandani's best man."

Aditya was totally confused 'What was the manager saying, how can it be so?' His thoughts made him restless. He took two days' emergency leave and left the office to take a taxi straight to Kolhapur.

"Well, we wanted to tell you this for a long time" said Dada, "we had lost the case against my brother, who got full custody of the company. He ruined the show and sold the almost bankrupt company to Mirchandani who knew me very well and gave me the manager's post. Actually we are no longer rich. We do not have any servants. We own only this house and I get a small salary."

Aditya was still in a state of deep shock, "When did all this happen?"

"It was when you started your MBA in Mumbai. We put a large portion of our savings to pay your second year's fees and to take care of your expenses. Then we asked you to take up a job for experience only to keep you away from this tragedy."

It took some time for Aditya to understand the plot. His grandfather was the stepson who had lost the case against the filial son who was a bad guy. They also did not let him come back when he didn't get the promotion, because actually there was no business that could be acquired.

"You talk so much about fighting, why did you not fight to get your business back?" asked Aditya.

"We lost our son, we lost our business. Old age is weakening our bones. We therefore decided to pass the baton on to you," he said "we decided to fight for your success because the probability of our victory was very low."

Aditya was happy to have such wise grandparents. They had never shared their grief with him at the same time trying to make him totally independent and successful. He sat down with his head buried on the table. A hand came on his head. It was Aai. She had tears in her eyes.

"Preparing a fighter for a fight is also fighting, my son. Leadership is all about teamwork and not just winning on one's own;" her words of wisdom always remained with Aditya, who retired at 60 as the global Managing Director of Acmeee International.

Notes

A Slap on Her Face

Slap, slap....It was a sharp and loud sound that she heard. It was followed by a loud cry from a little girl. It suddenly reminded her of her first memories of early childhood when her mother had similarly slapped her not once but twice.

She was sitting in a cafe, sipping her coffee and staring out the window. On the opposite table, a small girl had come with her mother. She wanted iced tea. But her mother was firm and asked her not to have anything cold. The girl started crying for iced tea. She made a scene by yelling. Her mother got up and slapped her twice.

The sound of the slap rattled Riya. It took her back thirty years when she had also been slapped by her mother. Her only mistake had been to ask for a hard boiled candy costing fifty paisa. Her mother didn't have even a single naya paisa to spare. She used to live in utter poverty and was totally frustrated with life. Her only option had been to give her two tight slaps. The objective was to kill all such requests in the coming days and that would have been all the more difficult.

Children's minds are clean and pure. Our harsh actions make permanent scars. These slaps too had been instrumental in changing Riya's mindset.

As a child, she was so innocent, so vulnerable and so pure. Today, she was a criminal. Not just an ordinary criminal wanted internationally but a murderer. As she sipped her cappuccino, she started thinking about her journey that had begun in innocence in childhood and had led to her to becoming a hardened criminal in adulthood. Her whole life began to flashin front of her eyes.

Riya was born into a family that existed below the poverty-line. Her father was an auto-rickshaw driver and her mother worked in many homes as a house maid. They lived in the slums of Ghatkopar, a suburb of Mumbai. She had grown up in a very tough environment. As a child she always visited the local garden near her house. Other children used to come there, playing with toys, arriving in cars, buying balloons. She had been deprived of all the good things in life. Asking her parents for any of these good things could lead to a slap. She felt sad.

Her grief and the slaps had created strong desires. These desires were like a devil within her and it was becoming difficult to control that devil as the days passed by. The local municipal school was free for girls. It did not have good teachers or other facilities but was run by some social workers. They made efforts to ensure that children got an education till at least class 10.

Riya was good at studies and good at drawing. She was a born artist. Her parents were keen on educating Riya. They did not leave any stone unturned to ensure that she did her schooling properly. She scored very good marks in the state board 10th standard examination. With funding from some relatives and friends, she could join a college to obtain a diploma. At 19, she was selected as a Visualizer in a mid-scale advertising company.

She was good at her work. Her colleagues and boss appreciated her performance. They knew that Riya would become big one day. Her salary increment was the highest. Riya was a successful employee. Her parents were very happy that their daughter had achieved something very big in life. They were proud of her performance and always spoke highly of her to all.

Riya was however still an unsatisfied and hungry soul. She was not going to settle for an ordinary salary. She wanted to make a lot of money. Everybody wants to make money, everybody wants to buy a car, a house, have a good bank balance, but in a correct manner and at the right time. This was not the case with Riya. She was not willing to wait.

At 22, Riya met Kabir. He was a vendor supplying exhibition equipment. He also executed the erections of stalls. Riya and Kabir worked as a team. Riya's designs were excellent and Kabir's execution capacity was above average. The sales team regularly picked up a number of repeat orders due to their work.

With work, Riya and Kabir came closer. They had a very strange relationship. It was not exactly love or friendship but their thoughts matched very well. They both worked at the same frequency. It was not long before Riya found herself in Kabir's bed.

Kabir, a young businessman from an erstwhile rich family, was keen to make his mark in the industry. Kabir was born with a silver spoon in his mouth but his father had lost most of his wealth in horse-racing and gambling. His father's final attempt to save the ancestral property in south Mumbai was the last of his failures before he committed suicide in his mansion. The family now lived in 1BHK apartment in Virar.

Both families were opposed to their relationship. Riya and Kabir decided to break family ties. They left home and moved into a rented one room flat. Live-in relationships were a strict no-no for which their families refused to have any relations with them.

The super-efficient couple decided to hold hands and work on their own. Riya quit her job to join Kabir. They were able to pull a few good accounts. Their delivery was good and repeat orders started falling in. On completion of the first year, the Riya-Kabir association managed to secure a business of 50 lakhs with a decent profit of 7 lakhs.

There is a relationship between success, desire and greed. If success after success leads to reduction of desire, there is not much greed involved. However if success and desire grow proportional to each other, the result obviously leads to a rise in greed.

The train of greed is pulled by the engine of success. The bogies now develop a momentum of their own. They will not slow down even if the engine's power gets reduced. The result has to be an accident due to no reduction in speed. This accident gives birth to evil and evil is defintely a source of crime, isn't it?

House, car, wealth would have to wait for at least 5-7 more years. Both Riya and Kabir were not in a mood to wait. Increase of capacity would lead to addition of resources and initial reduction of profitability. They now therefore needed an idea that would lead to more and more money.

The business scenario was booming. A very big exhibition was on its way. Clients were keen to work with this couple. Riya wanted double the orders. She wasn't happy getting only repeat orders and wanted huge orders from new clients as well.

Both minds became busy. Kabir struck upon a flawless plot. He discussed it with Riya. She was initially uncomfortable, but when Kabir showed her the projected profits the figures made her change her mind. Evil having been conceived was knocking on greed's doors to be delivered.

They spent the full week in preparing the plan, making contacts, getting associated with petty criminals, making fake documents etc. The duo offered an excellent proposal to all their existing and new clients. The job was to design and execute exhibition stalls for all their clients. All other vendors offered a blanket price which was all inclusive. Kabir's proposal was different. It had a break up of material, labour and management fees. They had also mentioned the names of two material suppliers and one labour contractor. The clients had to make a payment in advance to these 3 parties. The overall responsibility was with Riya and Kabir. They assured the client of a single-point contact. The transaction ensured that the overall cost to the client was reduced due to multiple vendor payments. This would help Riya and Kabir show lower incomes and accordingly pay reduced taxes. The best part was that the overall cost to a client was the lowest. The client was also assured of getting the best quality material at a reasonable price.

The proposal was accepted by many existing and new clients. The past reference list was clean. Many clients agreed and the Order book for this single exhibition crossed 40 lakhs. The condition was that 50% of the money had to be paid in advance before the exhibition.

Sadly all the three vendors were fictitious. The money was transferred into accounts of non-existent companies. The documentation was made by Kabir's contacts in crime and the money withdrawn by his henchmen.

A week before the exhibition, the couple visited all their clients and informed them about the fake vendors. They declared bankruptcy and offered a written communication, owning full responsibility. They also promised to return the advance taken from clients. Considering the past experience, and reference checks, all the clients sympathized with the couple. They accepted the written confirmations. With very few days remaining for the exhibition, most of the clients decided to go with them and once again paid them the full amount. Riya and Kabir left Mumbai forever just two days before the exhibition with 50 lakhs in cash. The clients were shocked. The fraud had been unveiled. Police complaints were made. But it was too late. The couple was now in Bangalore with fake names and passports. Riya had cut her hair short and had boyish looks now. Kabir was clean shaven now and had grown a moustache. It wasn't easy to recognize any of them. The Mumbai police was clueless. They only managed to harass both families who were already in grief.

The city of Bangalore was flourishing. Riya managed to get a job in a shopping mall. The mall had many shops. More than 500 boys and girls worked in the mall. During her work, Riya made many friends. Kabir was introduced as a Dubai-based business man. This time each one stayed separately. They did not want to invite trouble by being together for the police were on the lookout for a couple.

Kabir offered a savings scheme to all the employee of the Mall. Riya managed to publicize the same orally. She swore on the genuineness of the scheme and would show some expensive gifts she had managed previously through the profits that she had made by handing over her savings to Mr. Kabir.

In this scheme, the customers had to deposit an amount on the first day of the month and would get three times the bank interest by the end of the month. It was difficult in the beginning for employees to believe, but Riya managed to convince them. Those few gullible enough tried it by depositing small amounts. Our couple had cash in hand and they could easily pay back the amount with interest. These happy recipients not just doubled their investments but also recommended the scheme to their friends. Riya now had a few more people spreading the business by recommending Kabir.

Many mall employees started depositing huge amounts of money. Most of them did not ask for refunds and kept adding more money every month for a greater recurring effect.

Riya and Kabir had by now spent about 12 lakhs in just interest that had been paid to employees. Their trap was well set. The time had now come for the final blow. They stopped all small schemes and set up a single 6-month recurring scheme that would lead to a handsome pay-out on Diwali with bonus. The public were excited. They also did not need any security because they had seen their money grow. Kabir had informed them about a Dubai investor who had been giving them the interest. He also used to frequently travel to Dubai.

The scheme was set. This time, not just the employees of the mall, but many others also invested. In five months, our partners in crime had Rs. 3.5 crores which were then secretly transferred to different accounts in Dubai through their syndicate. Riya had prepared letters on bonus amounts and refund dates to all investors. These letters were couriered to their houses along with a big box of chocolates. The investors were delighted. It was however the last time they would be experiencing happiness related to their hard-earned money. Soon they found that it was a fraud but could do nothing because both Riya and Kabir had flown out to Dubai on fictitious passports.

The money was converted to dirham. The criminal syndicate was efficient. All arrangements had been meticulously made for the couple, including their marriage certificate. This time they were Mr. and Mrs. Khan.

Their partners in crime had a lot of support for the intelligent couple. Their investments had paid off and their partners were now willing to invest huge amounts of money in the new game.

The next idea was completely web based. They floated a company called Market Research Syndicate (MRS). This company was in partnership with a local Pakistani citizen,

Altaf. It was registered in India under a fake address. The idea was simple. They hired web experts to design and launch a web portal. This portal invited membership from all citizens of India. A member paid 21,111/- rupees to register and an annual fee. This member would now have to log in every weekend and fill up a market survey form. This survey could be about any product. Each successful completion would give them 100 rupees. The web portal would be offering 10 to 15 survey forms per weekend. The total potential earning per member per annum was estimated to be Rs. 55000. The site would also announce bonuses subject to market situations. They appointed a CEO in Delhi who engaged a full time agency. This agency purchased primetime television slots to market the web portal.

Television advertisements were effective within the first 3 months with the company making ten million members. Payments were made to them on a weekly basis. The members were delighted to receive the small payments and recommended the site to their family and friends. After making handsome payments to the Indian CEO, the basic staff, the web designers and the television commercials, this fake company put an end to the business. This game was big. The take-home for the criminals was Rs. 350 millions.

Riya and Kabir were now international criminals. They could no longer stay in Dubai. The police, CBI, FBI, DRI, and many others were hot on their heels. But the planning was foolproof. Altaf had already arranged a Pakistani visa for them. The trio was in Pakistan when the scheme was blown. The money was safe in Swiss banks.

With major crimes on their heads, Riya and Kabir spent the next one year in Pakistan. This was the time they got married. Luxuries were flowing. They had a palatial home, luxury cars, servants and a great lifestyle. Altaf helped them make friends with some of the best known criminals. They regularly attended parties that included some top film stars from Bollywood. Life was good. This is exactly what they had always wanted. They were successful.

They say that crime does not pay. It also does not leave you at peace. After a big one-year vacation, the duo was summoned by Altaf to Dubai. This time they were officially Pakistani citizens with different names. They attended a meeting with some of the top criminals of the world. The plan was dangerous. It disturbed both Riya and Kabir. They came out of the meeting and went back to their hotel room. Altaf visited them to find out why they had suddenly left the meeting.

"We will not work in any assignment which is for terrorism" screamed Riya. Altaf was shocked to see this reaction.

"Yes, Altafbhai, we will not participate in any such work. We are interested in making money but not by killing innocent people" said Kabir.

"How very unfortunate!" I had very big plans for you. Anyway since you have attended the meeting and have understood our plans, we cannot help it. Moving out is not an option any more. This will be your last project. I promise. Please do it" said Altaf.

"Get out Altaf. Never show us your face again" said Riya.

Altaf was upset. Kabir moved forward and opened the door for him. Altaf moved towards the door and closed it.

"The only option left for me is to kill you both. I am sorry. I liked you but I am sorry" said Altaf, as he pulled out his gun.

Riya was expecting this reaction. She was prepared for it. As Altaf pulled out his gun, she smashed a heavy solid-glass ashtray on his head. The ashtray hit him right on his nose. He yelled out in pain. Kabir moved fast and grabbed his gun and threw it out the window. Altaf got up and pulled out his knife. Kabir jumped on him. But Altaf was well trained for combat. He twisted Kabir's hand and struck the knife in Kabir's stomach.

Kabir fell flat on the ground. Altaf then moved towards Riya, who was in a state of shock. Altaf held her neck to suffocate her. Riya struggled but Altaf was too strong. Just before she fainted, Altaf screamed. He loosened his grip and flew down. It was Kabir. He had got up and stabbed him with the same knife before finally falling on the floor.

As Riya came back to her normal state, both Kabir and Altaf were lying dead in the room. Her mind was still blank. She sat down on the floor. Tears started rolling from her eyes. Kabir was dead. She then pushed both the bodies into the bathroom, took her purse, packed a small hand-bag and walked out of the hotel room with a "Do Not Disturb" sign on the door. A taxi brought her to the airport. She booked herself on the next flight to Pakistan. It left in the next 3 hours. The Dubai airport coffee shop was her next destination.

"One cappuccino please" she said to the boy standing at the counter. As she opened her handbag to pay, the knife wrapped in her scarf appeared on the top.

The little girl on the table facing her,, slapped by her mom, was still crying. Her mom went and kissed the girl. She took her in her arms and was consoling her baby girl. She was no longer crying. Both mom and baby were happily enjoying themselves. They were playing with each other, laughing loudly.

The mother and her baby were surprised to see a girl sitting on the opposite table burst into tears. She was crying out very loudly. The baby girl asked her mom "why is she crying?" The lady got up from her table. She sat next to Riya.

"Are you okay dear?" she asked Riya.

"Yes, I am alright, never felt better" said Riya.

She got up from her table and went directly to the Indian embassy to surrender. They flew her back to Mumbai. She gave her statement to the police. They gave her one final meeting with her parents before sending her to jail. She told them about the complete plan, the names of the terrorists and their destinations. The cash that was remaining was returned to the police. They treated her fairly. Her cooperation led to a reduction in her period of punishment..

After spending five years in jail, Riya is today working for the betterment of house maids. She helps them improve skills like cooking, maintaining expenses etc. Her mother is now very old but happy to see her get on in life.

After all, her slaps had brought Riya back....

Notes

A "Thank You" Note

The names listed below are of some good people who have contributed significantly to my life. I am taking advantage of this space and opportunity to thank them all and hope to continue networking with them.

Note: In case I have inadvertently missed anyone's name, please accept my sincere apologies. I assure you that it will be included in my next book.

Abhay Kardeguddi

Abhijit Som

Abhishek Pradhan

Ajay Ambewadikar

Ajay Chitnis

Ajit Pradhan

Ajoy Medhekar

Akansha Gupta

Ameya Randive

Amitabh Bhagwate

Amog Mathure

Amruta Karkhanis

Amruta Munde

Anand Bhandarkar

Anand Dantu

Anand Daptardar

Anand Kavi

Anil Martyris

Aparna Daptardar

Aparna Joshi

Aparna Sharma

Archana Joshi

Arun Karambelkar

Ashfaq Ahad

Ashish Hendre

Ashok Mehta

Ashwini Gaikwad

Ashwini Malpani

Atul Kale

Atul Nachne

Avijit Paul

AVR Murthy

BC Chatopadhya

BC Rao

Biren Bhuta

Chaitanya Sahastrabudhe

Chandrakant Salunkhe

Charu Mahagaonkar

Chirag Trivedi

Debabrata Sain

Deelip Amolic

Deepesh Deshmukh

Devashish Singh

Devdatta Mahiskar

Dhiraj Arora
Dinanath Bhanage
Dipanjan Ghoshal
Farooq Merchant
Gajanand Shende
Gautam Dighe
Govind Raju
Guru Tantry
Gurudatt Pandit
GVR Murthy
Hakan Kingstedt
Harendra Deshpande
Harshavardhan Bhave
Hemant Watve
Herbert Buder
Jauqline Sunny
Jyoti Sharma
Kaushal Mehta
Keval Sutar
Kirti Hadap
Kosaraju Chandrasekhar
Lee Kheng NG
Mahaboob Pasha
Mahesh Phanse
Mallika Gupte
Manish Chopra
Manoj Randive
Marie-Louise Ek
Minal Srinivasan
Monica Pradhan
Neil Antao
Nikhilesh Mehta

Nilesh Dixit
Nilesh Gupte
Nilesh Lalsare
Nilesh Porwal
Nimish Hadkar
Nimisha Iyer
Niranjan Rembhotkar
Nitin Thakkar
Pankaj Shrivastav
Parikshit Karnik
Pominder Kaur
Pramod Ranjan
Pranav Patankar
Prasad KVD
Prashant Ambulkar
Pravin Shimpi
Priya Philip
Priyanka Basu
Pv Krishnan
Raghavendra Joshi
Rahul Bose
Rahul Deshpande
Raj Shrivastav
Rajagopalan Paliyath
Rajendra Pradhan
Rajita Kumar
Ramana Kumar
Ramanand Sule
Ramesh Solanki
Rashmi Sagare
Ravi Vyas
Roger Jansson

Rohit Kapoor
Sachin Kotwal
Sachin Patil
Sagar Deshpande
Sameer Gupte
Sandeep Bhattacharjee
Sandeep Sharma
Sanil Solanki
Sanjay Ahuja
Sanjay Mahagaonkar
Sanket Solanki
Saptarishi Naha
Satya Raju
Shailesh Dhume
Shailesh Prabhune
Shalini Sharma
Shashiprakasha L.S.
Shehnaaz Chawla
Shib Bhomik
Shivakant Upadhyaya
Shivangi Page
Shrikanth Wavre
Simon Meester
Soumitra Banerjee
Srinivasa Raghavan

Subhasis Das
Subir Chatterjee
Subodh Chavan
Sudhir Shrivastav
Sudhir Sohni
Sudhir Udapurkar
Supriya Durve
Surendra Sahoo
Sushma Solanki
Swapnil Chaubal
Swati Telang
Tanuja Donde
Topor Basu
Uday Randive
Ujwal Kunte
Varsha Dighe
Vikram Deshpande
Vinay Pande
Vinayak Deshmukh
Vinayak Wagh
Vinod Malpani
Vinod Sisodia
Vrushali Kumar
Yashodhan Deshmukh
Yogesh Raje

They say that when you want to achieve something
desperately,
the entire universe tries to deliver it to you

– Taken from Paulo Coelho's The Alchemist.

About the Author

Mandar Chitre has over 20 years of experience across the marketing domain, in top multinationals and leading Indian companies, with major business turnarounds under his leadership. He graduated in engineering from Pune and did his masters in marketing management from Mumbai. Mandar lectures at several management institutes across Mumbai and is sought for his qualifications in the legal and indirect tax arena. A keen writer, Mandar coaches young entrepreneurs because he enjoys sharing his experience with aspiring individuals and believes strongly in giving back to society. His articles have won awards in the contests conducted by TOI Ascent. He is a business consultant focused on solving complex situations, augmenting growth and training.

You can contact the author on mandarchitre@rediffmail.com

www.ingramcontent.com/pod-product-compliance
Lightning Source LLC
Chambersburg PA
CBHW031931190326
41519CB00007B/483